A *Tip* in the Right Direction

Positive Insights to Help You Learn and Grow

Robert A. Rohm, Ph.D.

Foreword by Billy Florence

III

THIRD BOOK IN THIS SERIES

A *Tip* in the Right Direction

Positive Insights to Help You Learn and Grow

Personality
INSIGHTS

Robert A. Rohm, Ph.D.

Published by Personality Insights, Inc.

P.O. Box 28592 • Atlanta, GA 30358-0592

1.800.509.DISC • www.personalityinsights.com

ISBN: 0-9741760-9-5

Table of Contents:

This book is affectionately dedicated to my four daughters: Rachael Rohm Gelinas, Esther Rohm Thompson, Elizabeth Rohm Carroll and Susanna Faith Rohm. These four, precious girls have done more to influence and shape the direction of my life than any other people in the world. Almost everything good I truly know and understand deep down inside my heart, I learned by being their father.

Life is a most interesting teacher. It is also very patient. If at first you do not learn the lesson life is trying to teach you, it will soon send you other opportunities to learn the same lesson again...and again until you finally learn what life wants you to know. Each daughter has done a masterful job of teaching me different lessons.

Rachael has taught me how to succeed at anything I attempt. She dislikes failure more than anyone I know. She is my "Tiger," staying on the hunt and attack until any job she approaches is complete!

Esther has taught me how to have fun. She has kept me young at heart. I have never laughed so much with any other person as much as I have with her. She has made my heart happy!

Elizabeth has taught me kindness and gentleness. She is one of the sweetest people I have ever known. She has shown me what unselfishness and forgiveness are all about. What a great heart she has!

Susanna has taught me how to be real. There is not a "fake" bone in her body. She deals with every situation or issue as it arises. She has shown me the power of learning to listen to my own feelings. What a wise counselor she has become!

I have been unusually blessed in my life in many ways. I have made mistakes I wish I could "undo." But, nothing has been a greater blessing to me than the privilege of being the father of these four incredible girls I lovingly call my daughters.

Foreword

When Peggy and I began hosting our own business functions years ago, we met many interesting people. We soon discovered that some individuals have the unique ability to make you feel as if you had known them all of your life. Such was the case with Dr. Robert Rohm. The insightful information he shared began to clarify and crystallize many of the concepts we had already been exposed to in our business. However, no one had ever explained these concepts in such a simple, practical, understandable, usable and most of all, transferable manner! We immediately saw how his information would relate to the two key areas of our business and our lives; namely tasks and people.

I am more task-oriented, so my focus is on helping people reach their goals or accomplish their dreams. My wife, Peggy, on the other hand, is more people-oriented. She is a great at building relationships. She has the unique ability to make everyone she meets feel loved and accepted.

When you meet Peggy, you have just met your new best friend!

In Robert Rohm, we found someone who specialized in the two key areas in which Peggy and I were interested: tasks and people. He began to teach us the D-I-S-C Model of Human Behavior. The people in our organization loved the information and they loved Dr. Rohm! (His use of humor and facial expressions keeps the audience alert while he teaches. It is a fascinating process to watch.) Over the years he has become a dear friend and an important part of our business development team.

This "Tip" book is Volume 3 in a series of books entitled, "A Tip in the Right Direction." These books are packed with common sense approaches to life, business and relationships. It has been our experience in working with people that if you possess good information, you will find yourself in a better position to make wise choices in life. This book contains that kind of good, wise information.

Peggy and I hope you will read these pages over and over and gain much insight into how to succeed in every area of your life. There is an old saying, "If you put good food on the table, people will come and eat!" The table has been set for you in this book. Come and eat!

Billy Florence, President
Florence Enterprises, Inc.
Dream Chasers International, Inc.
Athens, Georgia

Acknowledgments

I want to thank my staff (whom I affectionately call "my team") for all of the help that each one has given me in creating this work. My editor, Beth McLendon, spent countless hours working on the flow of the book so that it makes sense. Because the spoken word and the written word is so different, Beth often went far beyond the call of duty in reworking my thoughts to ensure that everything is grammatically correct. Beth has been our staff eagle!

I want to thank Pedro Gonzales, our Art Director, for creating a format for this book that is easy to read. Pedro is so gifted and creative. He is such a valuable asset to our Personality Insights Team.

I especially want to thank all the IBO's (Independent Business Owners) who have been the driving force in keeping me alert, and always on the lookout for new material and helpful ideas. Their desire to learn and grow is the kind of stuff from which greatness occurs. Their hunger for more information that helps them maintain good, positive mental attitudes gives them the edge needed to become the leaders this world so badly needs and so richly deserves. IBO's, never give up on your dreams!

Finally, but most importantly, I want to thank God for giving me fresh, new ideas each week to write about in the "Tips." I am sometimes fearful that I will eventually run out of good material. I am simply not all that creative.

However, God is creative, so I will continue to rely on Him as my primary resource. Thank you, Father! You are so good to me...and many others as well. We love and appreciate your faithfulness to all of your children.

A *helpful "Tip"*
before reading this book:

Many of the tips found in this book relate to the *DISC* Model of Human Behavior. In order for you to be up-to-date and current in your understanding of the information in this book, we thought it would be helpful to provide you with a brief overview of the Model of Human Behavior before you begin.

GET THE PICTURE

Most people have predictable patterns of behavior and specific personality types. There are four basic personality types, also known as temperaments. The four types are like four parts of a pie. Before looking at each of the four parts, let's look at the pie in two parts. These two parts are designated as **outgoing** and **reserved**. Think of it this way: some people are more outgoing, while others are more reserved.

Outgoing people are more active and optimistic. *Reserved* types are more passive and careful. One type is not better than the other. Both types of behavior are needed, and both are important. Outgoing types need to learn how to be more steady and cautious. Reserved types need to learn how to be more dominant and inspiring.

There is another way to divide the pie. It can be divided into *task-oriented* and *people-oriented*. Some people are more task-oriented, and some are more relationship-oriented.

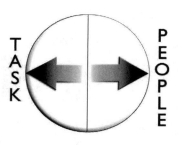

Task-oriented types need to learn to relate better to others and become more interactive and sharing. *People-oriented* individuals need to learn to be more focused on doing tasks or things. They need to be more directing and correcting.

Now, we can have a pie divided into four parts. We can visualize the four parts: *D*, *I*, *S* and *C*. Those people who we say are predominately *"D"* types are outgoing and task-oriented. Those who we say are predominately *"I"* types are

outgoing and people-oriented. Those who we say are predominately "*S*" types are reserved and people-oriented. Those who we say are predominately "*C*" types are reserved and task-oriented.

The "*D*" type can be described with words like: Dominant, Direct, Demanding, Decisive, Determined and Doer.

The "*I*" type can be described with words like: Inspiring, Influencing, Inducing, Interactive, Impressive and Interested in people.

The "*S*" type can be described with words like: Supportive, Steady, Stable, Sweet, Sensitive and Status Quo.

The "*C*" type can be described with words like: Cautious, Calculating, Competent, Consistent, Contemplative and Careful.

D = Dominant
I = Inspiring
S = Supportive
C = Cautious

No one is purely a "*D*" or an "*I*" or an "*S*" or a "*C*". Everyone is a unique blend of these four types. If someone says that he is an "*I* / *D*" personality blend, that means that he is highest in the traits of the "*I*" (Inspiring type), and that he is next highest in the traits of the "*D*" (Dominant type). This, of course, is true of the other traits, as well.

Robert A. Rohm Ph.D.

Introduction

I have heard that it takes twenty-one days of repetitive behavior to form a "habit". I know from first hand experience that good habits are wonderful assets to one's life. I also know that bad habits can cause extreme difficulty and be very stressful!

Several years ago I began writing a "Tip of the Week". In the beginning, it seemed as if every time I turned around, another week had passed and it was time to write another Tip. I trained my mind to look for interesting thoughts and concepts that meant a lot to me and had helped me in my daily life. In time, I developed one of the best habits I have ever acquired. The actual habit of writing a Tip each week caused me to open my eyes to my environment and the important issues that were taking place around me. As it turned out, most of the thoughts that developed into "Tips" were daily, common sense ideas.

These simple thoughts were sent by e-mail to business associates, family and friends. I never imagined the response I would receive! I soon discovered that my articles were being sent by recipients to their friends and associates. In time I received e-mails written by total strangers from all over the world telling me how much the "Tips" were appreciated. I was deeply touched by the recurring theme that they were practical and useful common sense ideas.

I do not know exactly when I fell in love with common sense. But, the older I get the more clearly I see that common sense is not all that common. I also have come to understand that common sense does not equal common practice! I am grateful for scholarship and the mountains of deep intellectual information that makes our world a better place. But, I am also grateful for "horse sense" because I see how valuable it is to our daily lives. I once heard Dolly Parton say, "I never did that well in school so I tried to develop some common sense to get me through life." Considering the fact that she has built the second most visited theme park in the world (after Disney World), I would have to say that having common sense has proved valuable to her!

I trust these "Tips" will provide you with new ideas, insights, and fresh common sense that will help you in all you do!

Thank you and God bless you!

Robert A. Rohm Ph.D.

1

If you want to take off with people, put in the right fuel!

As most of you know, I have a real passion for the topic of personality styles. I have made that one topic my life's pursuit. You have also probably heard me say, "If I understand you and you understand me, doesn't it make sense that we can have a better relationship?" I believe that is very true. But, have you ever taken the time to boil down the topic of relationships to its most basic truth? I believe the key to happy relationships, knowing how to communicate well and successful leadership is directly related to how well you get along with other people.

It is a fact, people will not go along with you until they get along with you. That leads us to the key question in this tip, namely, "Do you know how to get along with people?" Or, do you unknowingly have the attitude, "I want other people to get along with me!" There is a huge difference between those two questions.

If you want to get along well with other people, you must know the basic drive or motivation behind each personality style. When you know what "fuels" each type, you will be able to more successfully connect with them by providing their core desire. Just in case you have not committed these basic drives to memory, I will provide them for you once again.

The basic drives/motivations/"fuels" of each of the four personality styles:

"*D*" types – Results and success
"*I*" types – Fun and excitement
"*S*" types – Peace and harmony
"*C*" types – Quality answers, value, being correct

If you honestly and effectively put forth the effort to connect with individuals by using this technique, I guarantee you will be able to better get along with other people! However, it is important to use this technique in a genuine, heartfelt manner, instead of a mechanical way.

When you help "create a climate" for each of the four styles that motivates them, they, in turn, will want to be around you. In other words, when you try to "get along" with people, they will want to "go along" with you! The following quick example might help you. I have a good friend who is a high "*D*" type. When I meet with him, I am always on time or a little early. I try to let him lead the conversation and tell me what is on his mind. I usually ask questions to help clarify his goals, dreams and desires. We talk about how to get good results and success in every area of our life: relationships, finances and even our spiritual life. We always connect! Is it any wonder? Those are all the things he loves. When we are finished talking, we usually go to a movie or out to eat. That is what I love!

This really isn't rocket science... it is simply learning how to provide what other people want deep down inside. In other words, it is learning to "fuel" other people's needs.

This week, start putting forth some effort to "feed" people the emotional fuel they need in order to connect with them. If you want to be the one to build strong relationships with other people, the ball is "in your court" to put forth the effort. You will soon experience the rewards for all of your labor. You will be a person who truly blesses the lives of a lot of other people.

*Tip: If you want to take off
with people, put in the right fuel!*

Be a Reverse Tornado!

From 1981 to 1988, we lived in Dallas, Texas. It was quite an experience. I came to love Texas. Until you live there, you really cannot understand Texas. The whole state is like a high school pep rally. . . "We're number one!" While I was there, I learned why they say, "You can always tell a Texan...you just can't tell them much!"

Part of the state of Texas is located in "tornado alley." This is the strip of land that runs through Kansas, Oklahoma and Texas where many tornados occur. A tornado is a deadly storm. It destroys everything in its path! I have only seen one tornado face-to-face in my life. It is a nasty-looking creature and sounds just as terrible. Its nature is death, destruction and devastation.

Recently, I saw a T.V. special on the weather channel about tornados. (Can you believe some people actually chase them?!) The program showed how quickly a tornado appears, how much damage it creates and how quickly it is gone. As I watched the program, I realized what I want to do in my life! I want to be a reverse tornado!

As I mentioned earlier, a tornado has a single purpose – namely, to destroy everything in its path. What if you and I could be a reverse tornado? Rather than destroying everything that we came into contact with, we would build it up. We would help it and make it better than it was before our encounter with it. Rather than death, we would promote healing and life; rather than destruction, we would promote optimism and encouragement; rather than devastation, we would promote restoration and productivity. Wouldn't that be wonderful? The odd thing about this "fantasy" way of thinking is that it is actually possible! Every day, you and I can choose to be a reverse tornado.

A tornado thinks, "What can I do today to show little regard for anything in my path, and how can I be as destructive as possible?" (We all have known people like that, and they leave their mark wherever they go.)

I am suggesting that we choose to follow the opposite path. We can choose to build up rather than destroy by bringing encouragement, help and a positive outlook to everything we encounter. It begins with a mental picture of how you view your life. I believe if you get up each day and have the right attitude, then the building process can be a daily, ongoing process. For example, "What can I do today to improve every situation that I encounter?" When you do that, you will find that is exactly what will happen!

This week, get a mental image of a tornado coming toward you. Then look at it, and tell it to put itself in reverse! Then you join in, and experience the power of moving with it in a whole new direction with a whole new purpose!

Tip: Be a Reverse Tornado!

3

Life is like working in a firehouse.

There is a new movie out in theaters called *Ladder 49*. It is the story of a group of firefighters and how their lives interact with one another. Because of the nature of their work, they spend a lot of time together. Their families get together for birthdays and for other celebrations as well. Basically, the movie is a good portrayal of how a firefighter lives and what he or she does on the job.

I enjoyed seeing the movie. As I was later thinking about the movie, I noticed that life is a lot like working in a firehouse. First, there is a lot of preparation and training. A fire has a mind of its own, so you must be prepared to know what to do in a variety of situations. Second, fighting a fire requires a lot of teamwork. It is not something one person is designed to do. It is a team effort. Third, fighting a fire requires a chief, someone who will quickly make the hard decisions that are in the best interest of all concerned. Fourth, firefighters realize that a fire is coming. The question is not "IF," but "WHEN." Therefore, firefighters are anticipating the event, not surprised by it.

Many other analogies could be drawn, as I am sure you can imagine. However, to me, the most striking similarity of why life is like working in a firehouse is because nothing is really important until the bell goes off. All the training, organization, preparation, teamwork, planning, equipment and know-how in fighting a fire must be actually applied in order for any of it to be very useful. When the bell goes off, the real test of everything a firefighter knows becomes apparent. Life is like that.

In life, you can know it is important to be nice and respectful to other people, but can you do it when someone rubs you the wrong way and your bell goes off? You can know all about money and financial principles, but can you apply that knowledge when you see a great deal and want to spend a large part of your savings and your bell goes off?

In life, you can know all the principles of teamwork and the importance of family relationships, but can you be loving and accepting of other family members when they don't act the way you think they should and your bell goes off? Can you talk to people who have a different political or religious view from you and still be accepting of them as people, even though they let you know that they disagree with your point of view or belief system, when your bell goes off?

In life, you can know it is important to marry "for better or worse...until death do you part," but can you continue to work at it and fulfill that vow when the bell goes off, or were those simply meaningless words and another broken promise?

In life, you can know that drinking too much and drug abuse will help you reach an early grave, but what happens when you get around your friends and the pressure sets in and your bell goes off?

In other words, the real rubber hits the road and reality sets in when the bell goes off. Up until that happens, everything else is simply talk...and as my father used to say, "Talk is cheap!"

This week, try to view *Ladder 49*. Notice all the effort and everything that goes into being a firefighter. Then watch what happens when reality sets in and the bell goes off. At that point, everything changes...everything! Life and death, happiness and sadness, fulfillment and emptiness, and joy and grief are ultimately at stake, not only in the firefighter's world but in your world and mine as well. But, we won't really find that out until our bell goes off. . . will we?!

Tip: Life is like working in a firehouse.

4

Be a champion!

"Motivation is like deodorant – you need to constantly reapply it, because it wears out! Inspiration is completely different. Inspiration comes from the inside - from your heart, from your soul. Inspiration doesn't wear out."

Ruben Gonzalez[1]

R uben Gonzalez is a name that many people do not recognize. Ruben is a three-time Olympian in the sport of luge. When I first heard about the "luge," I had no idea what it was. Although I had seen it many times, I did not know what it was called.*

As Ruben was growing up, he was not known as a gifted athlete. He didn't take up the sport of luge until he was 21. Against all odds, four years later, he was competing in the Winter Olympics. At the age of 39, he was racing against 20-year-old participants in the Salt Lake City Olympics! Getting started late in life didn't affect Ruben's determination. He pursued his goals and became a remarkable three-time Olympian. Ruben's story inspires

---

* The luge is that part of the Winter Olympic sports where an individual comes down a snow - covered chute. The individual is lying on his or her back and is literally flying. The person who has the fastest time down the chute is the winner.

me to seek to get in the game of life, and not simply stay on the sidelines.

I had the opportunity to meet Ruben Gonzalez at a business function. He is quite a character. He has written something called the "Champion's Creed." He gave me a copy of it, and I would like to share it with you.

"The Champion's Creed"

I am a champion.
I believe in myself.
I have the will to win.
I set high goals for myself.
I surround myself with winners.
I am cool, positive and confident.
I have courage. I never give up.
I am willing to pay the price of success.
I love the struggle and the competition.
I stay relaxed and in control at all times.
I focus all my energy on the job at hand.
I vividly imagine what victory will feel like.
I am a champion, and **I will win.**

When I read the creed, I realized why Ruben Gonzalez has gone to the Olympics three times. He has trained his mind to be stronger than his body. It would be difficult for his body not to cooperate with someone who is thinking like Ruben thinks. What I am saying is both accurate and biblical! Our bodies should be under the control of our mind. As Proverbs tells us, "For as he (a man) thinketh in his heart, so is he."*

Now I realize that someone may read this and think, "Well you just cannot do something simply because your mind tells you that you can." And, that is true. However, most of us are light-years away from having our mind be too strong. I believe our mind can always use exercise, and like any good muscle, it can get stronger if we will simply use it.

This week, let me encourage you to review the "Champion's Creed." Read it over several times, and see if you can gain insights and strength. I know I have.

It is a slippery slope to begin thinking harmful, hurtful, negative thoughts. It is an important challenge to think good, positive thoughts every day. Every one of us will face this challenge throughout his or her life. Those of us who choose to follow the path that Ruben Gonzalez has set for us will be following in the steps of an Olympian. That sounds like a good idea to me!

Tip: Be a champion!

* Proverbs 23:7a KJV

5

There is a big difference between materialism and prosperity.

How many times in your life have you been warned not to be materialistic? You have often heard, "The love of money is the root of all evil."* Therefore, anything that is associated with money or "worldly wealth" is often looked down upon. This can become a very confusing issue. And the phrase about "loving money" is also greatly misunderstood. On one hand, we all need money, so we can survive. (I like what Zig Ziglar says, "Money isn't everything, but it is pretty close to oxygen!") On the other hand, if we do not conquer our passion for money, pretty soon everything we own will end up owning us! Again, I believe it is a bigger challenge than most of us realize.

Prosperity is different from materialism. It creates a mind-set of abundance. Materialism says, "I cannot afford that!" Prosperity says, "How can I afford that?" In other words, prosperity sees unlimited potential and opportunity.

God did not create a universe with limited resources. If history has taught us anything, it has taught us that there is an abundance of material in the world. And, if we do start to run out, we can simply create new alternatives. Years ago, everyone thought that we would all cease to exist if we ran out of coal. Then someone came along and figured out how to use oil. I believe we are very close to seeing a whole new form of energy use by either solar power or hydrogen. (I just heard on the news this week that new cars being imported into the U.S. will get 60 miles to the gallon.) Therefore, since God created abundance, we can all experience prosperity. My part is simple; I need to focus on my own mind-set and see things from a different perspective.

Listen to conversations more closely this week. You will be amazed to hear the "scarcity" mentality of most people. Everywhere you turn, conversations and debates are all centered around the issue of materialism vs. prosperity. Even though people do not use those exact words, that is still the main issue.

Materialism says, "Hold on to what you have; play it safe; save for a rainy day. I had better look out for myself, because nobody else will be there to help me. Hard times are coming. We have tried everything, and there are no more possibilities and I will soon run out of everything!"

Prosperity says, "Let's look for new creative ways to do things. Let's take a chance; if we fail, at least we will have tried – besides we will learn a lot in the process. Tomorrow will be better than today. The future is bright;

there are an infinite amount of possibilities, and the best is yet to come!"

I believe materialism is evil and will keep you in darkness all of your life if you let it. Prosperity, on the other hand, is good and will help you walk in the light, discovering new ways to learn and grow.

This week, become more prosperity-minded. See the abundance that is all around you. Look for new ways to expand what you are doing. Realize the unlimited potential that is in yourself and others.

Tip: There is a big difference between materialism and prosperity.

* 1 Timothy 6:10

6

Be more considerate.

I travel a lot. I watch a lot of people. I am amazed by a lot of things I see. I have learned a lot by observing other people's behavior. I often ask myself the question, "Do I do that? Do I act that way?"

I do not think, for the most part, that people do things deliberately. I certainly do not believe that people are doing things against me. I believe they are doing things for themselves. But that is where the "rub" comes in. Oftentimes, people do not realize how inconsiderate they are being towards other people without even realizing it. I do not want to be that kind of person, and I am sure you do not want to be that way either!

There are three areas in which I believe we could all do better: The first area is on the road. Have you ever observed how people drive? The left lane is supposed to be for driving the speed limit or passing another vehicle. The right lane is supposed to be for vehicles wanting to go a little slower. I would guess from general observation that over half of all drivers have never been taught that information. Also, have you ever noticed that when someone needs to change lanes, rather than safely speeding up and merging over, some drivers slow down and even come to a complete stop in order to move over a lane? I have seen that happen on interstate highways! That is extremely dangerous to do on a road where everyone else is driving over 55 miles per hour. Think ahead and prepare to move over and merge safely without endangering the lives of everyone else.

The second area is cell phone use. I am amazed at people that sit right beside you on a crowded plane or in a restaurant and carry on a loud conversation as though they are the only one present. They act as if the person they are talking to cannot hear, because they are in a crowded room or a loud location. I have discovered the fact that you can put your hand over your mouth and almost whisper, and the person listening can hear just fine. Therefore, I encourage people to be more aware of voice volume.

Finally, the third area has to do with hallways, doorways and main walking areas. Every day people walk along and suddenly stop right in the middle of the traffic flow. It doesn't matter if it is in the airport, the mall or at church. It seems people are totally oblivious to the fact that they are creating a bottleneck condition for other people. All it takes is two seconds to move next to a wall or out of the main walkway in order to be considerate and let others more easily move around you.

I know you could possibly take this tip in the wrong

way. You could be thinking "Wow, Dr. Rohm, I had no idea everyone upset you so much!" Honestly, that is not my intent at all. Instead, I am concerned about my own politeness and the fact that I may be creating a hardship or frustration for someone else unnecessarily.

This week, pay closer attention to your driving manners, cell phone manners and walking manners. Learn as you observe the behaviors of others. That is usually the best teacher of all!

Tip: Be more considerate.

7

Stand up and speak!

Speaking in public has long been regarded as one of life's biggest fears. It has been reported that the average person's greatest fear in life is being burned to death by fire. The second biggest fear is public speaking.

It is difficult for me to relate to a person being afraid of public speaking. After all, I've been speaking in public, and enjoying the experience, basically all of my life! I began speaking when I was chosen as the Master of Ceremonies at my 5-year-old kindergarten graduation program. I still remember my speech: "Good evening, ladies and gentlemen. Welcome to the First Methodist Church kindergarten graduation program. We hope to present to you tonight our amateur efforts of *Goldilocks and the Three Bears*." I then introduced all of my classmates and the part each one would play. They were all dressed up in different costumes while I stood up in front before the whole audience dressed in a white tuxedo! That is when I fell in love with public speaking. It is also when I learned my favorite Bible verse – "There is no business like show business!" (I was just kidding about that being a Bible verse!) You can easily see my excitement and joy concerning public speaking!

Years later, in high school, I remember taking a speech class. My best friend, Champ Vance, sat right behind me. I can still remember how nervous he got before it was his turn to give a talk. He sweated all the way through his shoes, until the floor was actually wet underneath his shoes. That is the honest truth.

I had a difficult time understanding the fear of my friend, Champ. It was hard to relate to him and be sensitive to his fears. As I have grown and learned more about compassion and more about personality styles, I have developed a desire to become more sensitive to the fears of others who are less willing to speak than I am.

Even though I cannot easily empathize with a strong fear concerning public speaking, I can share some advice that I believe will help you view public speaking in a different light and thus reduce your fear. This tip was given by one of my college professors during a class lecture on public speaking. He taught us to begin by looking at our speaking topic and its importance. He told us to look to the audience's need to receive our information. He then used the "burning house" story. He told us that if he walked past our house at 2 o'clock in the morning and saw the roof of our house on fire, he would knock on the door to warn us and help us. His knowledge about information that we needed to hear would far surpass and overshadow his thoughts of how we might view him. He explained that many times we fall into the trap of giving more weight to the fear of how other people will view us, rather than to the idea that we could actually be helping others by giving them needed information. We could even fall into selfishness by withholding information that would help or bless others. Obviously in the "burning house" story, the height of selfishness would be someone leaving the neighborhood without knocking on the door and alerting the residents to vital information.

I never forgot that story. I now believe that when I stand up to speak, I have something important to say. I see my role as helping people. Therefore, I have learned to look past any fear that I feel and instead focus on the needs of the audience. It has always worked!

This concept also relates to sales. The best salespeople are the ones who have gotten past their fear of the presentation, and instead, focus on the value in the product being sold. They become other-centered instead of self-centered.

If you have a fear of speaking in public, let me encourage you and once again remind you that you are not alone. You are a unique and gifted person with important things to say. The world will be blessed when you stand up and speak. Nevertheless, I am not advocating that you jump into a situation that would cause you to panic. Instead, I am encouraging you to consider stepping out into opportunities in which you actually do feel uncomfortable. Situations in which you feel somewhat uncomfortable can be viewed as opportunities for potential growth. Consider doing one of the following:

1. Volunteer to help teach children in some capacity. Children have very low standards of perfection, and they are very forgiving.
2. Be open to opportunities to share an idea in a group setting. For example, in a work meeting or a Sunday school class.
3. Volunteer to make announcements at an organization where you are a member.

After you feel somewhat comfortable with those kinds of experiences, you may want to continue to reduce your speaking fears by doing more advanced public speaking:

1. Offering to teach a class in your religious organization where you are a member.
2. Taking a class on speaking that actually gets you up speaking in front of a group, like Toastmasters.
3. Looking for opportunities to actually practice speaking in public. In other words... just do it! That is the best way to learn.

I have been a public speaker for over 50 years! I have learned something valuable from every opportunity that I have had to speak. One day I will write a book on everything I have learned about public speaking. The conclusion of the book will simply be: overcome your own fears by focusing on helping other people!

I encourage you to find out how great it is to speak on a topic that helps other people. It feels wonderful to stand up, deliver your message and help people. I encourage you to do it soon!

Tip: Stand up and speak!

8

Rest!

For the past few days, I have had the opportunity to get some rest. I know that everyone needs rest on a daily basis, but sometimes we need to get some additional rest in order for us to recharge our batteries.

I believe in hard work, dedication and commitment. If you were to ask anyone that has spent very much time with me, they probably will tell you that I tend to be a workaholic. I believe in a strong work ethic, but I also know that life requires balance. The ability to slow down and get additional rest at times is greatly needed in order to fulfill the long-term goals, purposes and plans for my life. No one can operate on "full-blast" all of the time. The older I get, the more I see that life really is a marathon, not a sprint. However, at times, the ability to pace myself can be difficult. There is an old saying that I once read, "If you do not come apart and rest for a while...you will come apart completely!" I think that pretty much sums up what I am trying to say in this week's tip.

Many of us have the mind-set that we should work 50 weeks a year and take a couple of weeks off for vacation and rest. I would suggest that we add some rest into our daily schedule. I have discovered that rest is very healing. It allows me to be refreshed in order to think more clearly and make fewer mistakes. I understand that the airlines even have strict laws as to how many hours a pilot can fly before he or she has to have some downtime in order to rest. I assume that is because the airlines know that if a pilot is exhausted, he or she will be more prone to make errors in judgment or mistakes with the airplane. (As someone who flies a lot, I am grateful that the airlines have such a policy for their pilots!)

I believe our personalities come into play as we look at our attitudes towards work and rest. I am not picking on the "*D*" and "*I*" type personality styles, but both tend to be more outgoing and tend to overdo most everything. I really do believe that the "*S*" and "*C*" types could give us a little more help in learning to be more balanced in the area of rest. However, I also know that the "*S*" and "*C*" types, at times, should come out of their reserved state and "get after it" a little more. Again, all of this has to do with balance. One type is not right or wrong or good or bad. We are just different, and we need to help each other.

This week, let me encourage you to plan time for some good, old-fashioned rest. You may need to take a day off from work. At times, you might also want to consider getting into bed a little earlier at night. A football coach told me years ago that if you go to bed at an early hour when you are tired, your body will get better rest than it will if you go to bed late when you are overtired. I have found that to be very true.

Take care of your body. It is the only one you will ever get. It is important to exercise and feed it, but it is also important to let your body get some rest.

This week, I encourage you to take time to get rest.

Tip: Rest!

9

Not everything that counts can be counted, and not everything that can be counted counts.

The older I get, the more I see the difference between things that really matter in life and the things that do not matter. I have come to understand that relationships and the feelings of other people are much more important than paperwork. Most of the things that bog me down every day are the things that, in the long run, will not make much difference in my life or anyone else's life. Therefore, the things that I need to focus on are the things that really count.

We live in a world that is focused on "nickels and noses." Let me explain. When I was growing up in church, I noticed a sign on the wall in the sanctuary. It had two lines. The first line showed what the offering total was last Sunday and what the offering total was the same Sunday of the previous year. The second line compared the membership as of last week and the membership the same Sunday of the previous year. This was the origin of the phrase "nickels and noses." From this emphasis in our church, I got the impression that the two important things in church were how much money we had taken up and how many people were members. During all those years, the total offering and the total membership were the things that we counted every week, but in the long run, they were things that counted very little toward building a successful church.

I believe the same concept bleeds over into the business world. Years ago, I was spending some time with my mentor, Zig Ziglar. I told him I was having a very difficult time with the whole issue of money, because it seemed to permeate everything that I did. I told him that I did not want to be driven by money, but it seemed to be associated with every decision that I made. Zig explained to me some things that helped me very much. He said that my first priority should be helping people. My second objective should be to make a profit. And third, my goal should be to please God. Then he said something that I will never forget. He said that if you focus your priority on helping people, you will never have to chase money, because money will start chasing you. That was over 10 years ago, and I can honestly say that the truth of the concept that he taught me that day has proven to be very true. As long as I live every day of my life trying to focus on helping as many people as possible, money becomes a secondary issue. Again, it is impossible to count how many people you help on a daily basis, but in the long run, helping people is what really counts.

Human beings are funny creatures. We want to measure almost everything we do - our calories, our bank account, our height, our weight, our savings plans, how much time it is going to take to complete a project, how much gasoline costs per gallon, what our grocery bill is, how much is our monthly budget, etc. I am not diminishing those things, because it is very important to keep numbers as they relate to our daily life. None of us can live a very effective life, if we do not pay attention to the numbers. However, we must stop and ask ourselves, "Are we trying to count everything because we believe those are the things that really count in life, or have we learned to focus on the things that really count in life, which again, sometimes cannot be counted?"

This week, why not step back and look at your own life and situation. I wrote the title of this week's tip on a 3x5 card several years ago. It has been a helpful reminder to me concerning my priorities and the way I live my life. I want to do the things that count, not only in this life but for eternity. I don't want to stay focused on counting everything, because I have discovered that most of it, in the long run, is stuff that does not matter and usually gets thrown out in the trash.

I will share one final story. I heard James Dobson talking about how he won a tennis tournament in the 1960's while he was in college at the University of

Southern California. After he won the tournament, the school put his trophy in one of the school's trophy cases. A few years ago, one of his friends noticed a dumpster full of trophies. He just happened to see the one that had James Dobson's name on it. It had been thrown in the trash! That is what usually happens to things that we think can be counted. We see our name on a trophy or something else that seems important, but twenty years later, we really discover if it was something that counted very little in life. I am grateful that Dr. Dobson has devoted his life to his Focus on the Family ministry. He believes that effort will count more than an old trophy in a dumpster in Southern California. I agree.

I hope that this week, each of us will re-examine the things we do each day, so that we can determine if they are things we are counting or things that really count!

Tip: Not everything that counts can be counted, and not everything that can be counted counts.

10

Expect the unexpected.

W e have been in our present location for two years. Recently, I was thinking back to January 2003. I remember when we packed up our Personality Insights office and moved to our new location. Several weeks earlier, we had spoken to our telephone service provider (MPower) in order to get all the phone lines and data service moved to the new location without any interruptions or problems. However, on the final day of our move, our communications provider, MPower, was bought out by Florida Digital Communication. That set off a chain of events that lasted for over a week. Our phone system and our DSL line went down, and no matter what I did… it would not get back up!

Now this may sound crazy, but I was not surprised when all of that happened! I am not claiming to be clairvoyant or anything like that. However, I do understand that the whole telecommunication business is in a state of "flux," and all of their systems are fragile and very sensitive.

I knew that we might be in for a bumpy ride!

Our voice message system changed daily in order to give updates. Our wonderful staff returned phone calls and messages on their cell phones for a week. It was stressful, but we made it through the process. Now everything is functional again. As far as I know, everybody who called our office was helped and no requests were late or lost.

The reason for this story is to remind you that one of Murphy's laws is true: If anything can go wrong, it will, and it will go wrong at the worst possible time. However, if you plan for the worst case scenario, you can more easily survive difficult situations. (All the passengers on the *Titanic* could have been saved if they had followed that principle. But they did not have enough lifeboats. After that tragedy, ships were required to have enough lifeboats for all the passengers. In other words, now they are required to "expect the unexpected!")

This week take some time to think about the situations in your life. Is something about to happen that could be prevented if you took a little time to take a closer look… at your car maintenance… at a relationship with a mate or child… at a business deal?

We all want good things to happen to us. That is perfectly normal. However, it might be wise to give this tip some thought. You may be glad in the long run that you did!

Tip: Expect the unexpected.

11

Raise your "C" traits.

The four personality styles are *"D"*, *"I"*, *"S"* and *"C"*. Everyone has some of each of the four personality styles. In my case, I have less *"C"* in me than any other style. Therefore, I do not naturally operate in the strengths of the *"C"* style. The *"C"* personality style is careful, cautious, conscientious, consistent, contemplative, organized, systematic, thorough, self-disciplined, accurate, precise, detail-oriented, logical and practical.

When I speak and write, I explain that my *"C"* traits are my biggest challenge. There is not a day that goes by that I do not try to work in that area. You see, I really do believe that some of the hidden secrets to my future success are in the area that I know least about. (I believe that is true for you as well!) We all need to learn and grow on a daily basis.

Recently, I read an article that "reemphasized" to me the importance of being careful to pay attention to details. I thought you might like a copy.

Strive for Perfection - Raise your "*C*" Traits!

If 99.9 percent is good enough, then...

- Two million documents will be lost by the IRS this year.
- 811,000 faulty rolls of 35 mm film will be loaded this year.
- 22,000 checks will be deducted from the wrong bank accounts in the next 60 minutes.
- 1,314 phone calls will be misplaced by telecommunication services every minute.
- 12 babies will be given to the wrong parents each day.
- 268,500 defective tires will be shipped this year.
- 14,208 defective personal computers will be shipped this year.
- 103,260 income tax returns will be processed incorrectly this year.
- 2,488,200 books will be shipped in the next 12 months with the wrong cover.
- 5,517,200 cases of soft drinks produced in the next 12 months will be flatter than a bad tire.
- Two plane landings daily at O'Hare International Airport in Chicago will be unsafe.

- 3,056 copies of tomorrow's *Wall Street Journal* will be missing one of the three sections.

- 18,322 pieces of mail will be mishandled in the next hour.

- 291 pacemaker operations will be performed incorrectly this year.

- 880,000 credit cards in circulation will turn out to have incorrect cardholder information on their magnetic strips.

- $9,690 will be spent today, tomorrow and each day in the future on defective, often unsafe, sporting equipment.

- 55 malfunctioning automatic teller machines will be installed in the next 12 months.

- 20,000 incorrect drug prescriptions will be written in the next 12 months.

- 114,500 mismatched pairs of shoes will be shipped this year.

- $761,900 will be spent in the next 12 months on tapes and compact discs that won't play.

- 107 incorrect medical procedures will be performed by the end of the day today.

- 315 entries in *Webster's Third New International Dictionary of the English Language* will turn out to be misspelled.

I realize that all the above examples could be viewed as extreme. However, they are also very realistic! I choose to try to do better in my life this week by growing in the area in which I am the weakest. How about you? Strive for Perfection - Raise your "C" traits!

Tip: Raise your "C" traits.

12

Review the 6 Rules For Being Human.

Recently, I read an article someone gave me. It had no author listed, so I cannot tell you who wrote it. Neither can I take credit for it; although I agree with every word of it. I wanted to share it with you, because it sums up so much of life in just a few sentences. Since I am a simple person, I like things simple. I believe many other people do as well.

6 Rules For Being Human*

1. You came with a body - it may not be the one that you would have chosen for yourself, but since you are stuck with it, treat it well.
2. You came with a mind - your mission is to fill it with something useful. Fortunately, the world is full of good teachers. Find some who can help you.
3. You cannot fail the tests of life - that's the good news. The bad news is that you get to keep taking the same

test over and over until you master it.

4. You will never quite catch on - the more you learn, the more you will realize how much you do not know.

5. You will never complete the journey - you want to get from here to there. But once you do, there becomes here, and you have to start all over again.

6. You are your own best teacher - you know more than the sum of your education. Trust your own instincts.

Although all 6 are important and true, I especially like number 5... "You will never complete the journey... once you get there, it becomes here, and you start over again." There is a lot of wisdom in that concept.

Our society teaches you to "get finished." Wisdom encourages you to continue on the journey. We all need to remember that!

This week, practice using the 6 Rules For Being Human. Focus on a different one each day, and see how life becomes more balanced. These rules make a lot of good sense. I need all the sense I can get!

Tip: Review the 6 Rules For Being Human.

*Author Unknown

13

If you want to know what a person is all about, do not listen to his words, instead, watch his actions.

As you know, our country is in the midst of a war with Iraq. This war is the direct result of the United States responding to the unprecedented attack that took place on our country on September 11, 2001. The U.S did not provoke this war, nor did it initiate it. The U.S. has simply responded, and then it did so only after months and months of trying to resolve matters in a non-violent manner.

I know that there are many different opinions about this subject and everyone is entitled to his or her own opinion. That is the definition of a free society. Healthy debate is the way to get the best ideas on the table and to arrive at the best solutions possible. However, in the midst of all of this, there is something very interesting taking place.

Have you been watching any of the rallies or demonstrations that have been taking place around America or in the world? I find it ironic that there is such a different atmosphere at these events.

Robert A. Rohm Ph.D.

Last week, I attended a "Pro-America" rally in Atlanta. The rally was all about supporting our troops, our leaders and our President. The rally was positive, upbeat and most of all peaceful. The speakers talked about their personal experiences with war. Many of the speakers had served our country in past campaigns (World War II, Korea, Vietnam and Desert Storm). They all talked about their dislike for war and the severe consequences it brought into their own personal lives. However, each one also talked about the necessity of defending freedom, liberty and life. Everyone at the rally was friendly, law-abiding and respectful. Families with children and their pets lined the sidewalks and the streets in order to show their support and unity for our troops and our country. Although the rally was not called a "pro-war" rally, it was evident that, because we faced war, if that was what it took, then we supported that decision. The "pro-war" rally was filled with peace!

When I got home, I turned on the T.V. and watched the news. The news reported on several so called "peace rallies" which have taken place around America and the world. At these peace rallies, there has been rioting, looting, fighting, injuries, attacks upon policemen, destruction of public property and arrests. I listened with interest at the venomous voice tones and belligerent words that I heard. I watched the actions and attitudes of the protesters as they let their point of view be heard. Their "peace rally" was filled with war!

My mind drifted back to the days of Dr. Martin Luther King, Jr. and the way that he led demonstrations for peace... in a peaceful manner. History has proven that the ones who were in the wrong in those days were the *violent* men and women (even some in authority). You see, in time, truth always prevails. The problem with many people is that they do not know how to discern what is taking place around them. They listen to words but fail to watch for actions.

This week, take a closer look at the actions of the people that you know. If a person cannot talk about a difficult topic in a thoughtful, rational, calm manner, it may be a sign that he or she has a deeper problem and is simply covering it up with BEING LOUD. Unfortunately, that technique has worked for years and will continue to work around people who are not wise and do not know how to think for themselves.

Tip: If you want to know what a person is all about, do not listen to his words, instead, watch his actions.

14

Be solution-oriented, not problem-oriented.

Have you ever noticed how easy it is to recognize a problem? Everywhere you turn, there is a problem. You either just got over a problem, you are in the midst of a problem facing you today or there is a new problem waiting for you just around the corner! That is not said in order to be negative or pessimistic. It is simply the truth.

I have been taught that I should learn to look at problems as challenges or opportunities, and I agree with that point of view. However, that is not the point that I am trying to make right now. Instead, in this tip, I am emphasizing that rather than "staring" at the problem, we need to learn to "look" for the solution. This is not a skill that many people possess. Most people would rather talk about the problem than talk about possible solutions. Why do you think that we have so many people in court? They want somebody to find their solution for them.

When I was a school principal, we had a small printing press in order to meet our in-house printing needs. One day, the man in charge of printing came to me and told me that the metal pin in the press had broken. He showed me the long metal pin, and he told me that the press would no longer work.

I walked over to the print shop with him to look at it. As we walked, he explained the problem to me over and over and over again. I know very little about a printing press, but I know how to look for solutions.

I asked him to get me a tenpenny nail. As he was getting the nail, he continued to tell me that the printing press was broken. I took the nail, and within 3 minutes, I had repaired the press by replacing the broken pin with the sturdy nail. The printing press was now back in operation.

If I live to be 100, I will never forget what he said to me next. He said, "How did you know how to do that?"

I replied, "I just learned today!"

We all had to take an I.Q. test when we were students in school. However, your I.Q. (Intelligence Quotient) is simply a number that reports how well you did on the test. Real intelligence has to do with how well you know how to solve problems. In other words, highly intelligent people have learned to find solutions. They have become masters at dreaming and thinking about what "might be" rather than what has always been. They know how to go about the task of getting things accomplished rather than simply complaining about the problem.

John F. Kennedy, quoting George Bernard Shaw said, "Other people see things and say: why – but I dream things that never were and say: why not."[2] In other words, anybody can see a problem, but it takes effort and thought to start looking for the solution.

If you learn to apply this tip, it will change the way you look at things. It will make you smarter, healthier and happier. It may even increase your financial income!

Tip: Be solution-oriented, not problem-oriented.

15

The only thing worse than losing your eyesight is losing your vision.

I remember a very sweet woman by the name of Catherine Estes. As a boy growing up in Griffin, Georgia, we would often pick Catherine up and give her a ride to church. She was always singing and talking or telling us about something exciting that had happened in her life that week. The thing that impressed me so much, even as a young man, was how positive and upbeat she was in spite of her limitation. You see, Catherine was blind.

Eyesight is a very precious gift. Over the years, my own eyesight has gotten worse. I can still see far away, but if it is up close, well, "Where are my glasses?"

It is one thing to not be able to see very well. It is quite another thing to not be able to see at all. Perhaps you have personally known someone who was blind. Catherine carried her big Braille Bible and songbook with her every time that we picked her up for church. I was amazed at her ability to read braille. Sometimes she would let me feel the writing. I can still feel her Braille Bible and songbook in my fingertips, even as I write this tip.

Catherine demonstrated by her actions something I would later come to understand. Helen Keller once said, "The only thing worse than losing your sight, is being able to see, but having no vision."[3] Most of us have heard that quote, but thanks to Catherine, I understand it. She never lost her vision for life. She sang in the choir, played the accordion, helped in the nursery, taught Sunday school and she never missed a service. (And for you "old timers," that meant Sunday morning, Sunday night and Wednesday night.)

For some reason, I never felt sorry for Catherine. I now realize it was because she would not let me, nor anybody else, feel sorry for her! She was focused on her vision of serving others. Being blind might have prevented her from driving a car, but it never hindered her from fulfilling her vision and purpose for living.

I would ask you to consider the current circumstances in which you find yourself. Have you lost your meaning and purpose for life? Maybe the reason things are not moving in the direction that you would like for them to move is because you have lost your vision. Do you still have goals and dreams that you would like to see come true?

This week why not clean off your "internal glasses" and clear up your vision. You will be glad you did.

Tip: The only thing worse than losing your eyesight is losing your vision.

16

The real key to life is faithfulness.

I n 1924, a young man named Gutzon Borglum was in South Dakota. He looked at a mountain of rock and saw something in his mind that no one else had ever seen. He made the comment, "American history shall march along that skyline."

It took him the next 3 years to get his project started. After assembling his team of helpers, he began the process of sculpting the images of George Washington, Thomas Jefferson, Abraham Lincoln and Theodore Roosevelt on the granite face of Mount Rushmore. Experienced miners worked under his supervision. Using dynamite and jackhammers, they removed 450,000 tons of rock.

In March 1941, shortly before the world's biggest sculpture was completed, Borglum died. Before his death, a newspaper reporter asked him what had been the hardest part of the project. Borglum replied, "The size of the task matters not. My job was to pick up the hammer every day."[4]

That is called faithfulness. Not many possess it. Oddly enough, anyone can, if he or she simply chooses to do so. Certain people stand out in history and we remember them, because they were faithful to "stick with what they knew was right."

Think about it. Paul was faithful to write the New Testament. How many people have been blessed because of his work? Peter was faithful to preach the Good News. How many people have been blessed because of his words? John was faithful to reveal the revelation God gave him of things to come. How many people have been blessed because of his wisdom? Today many people name their sons Paul, Peter or John.

On the other hand, Nero was the Roman emperor during the time that most of the New Testament was being written and distributed. He was faithful to no one, including his own people. Now people name their dogs Nero.

Faithfulness is hard. It is a lonely road. Not many people choose to travel that path. It is doing what is right day in and day out. . . even when you do not want to do so. But, oddly enough, it is on the road called faithfulness that you will find all of the blessings for which you are searching.

Everyone has heard of Thomas Edison's 2000 experiments that he logged in his journal when he was trying to figure out something called a light bulb. What was that really all about? You guessed it. . . faithfulness.

I have one last thought. I guess the reason it is on my mind is because I have a dear friend, 89-years-old, who is just about ready to step into eternity. I visited her at Emory Hospital recently. She has been the most faithful person that I have ever known in my life. Her whole life has been directed to trying to help other people, spiritually, financially and socially. I have seen it demonstrated in the lives of other people. It is a powerful character trait.

Do you know the only requirement God asks of us when we become His follower? It is faithfulness (see Matthew 25:14-23). Kind of simple, isn't it?

This week, think about faithfulness. Do you need to look at your faithfulness at work, in a relationship, a project, your health or your walk with God? At the end of the day, everything boils down to simply being faithful in all that we do. Rather than looking at an issue you face, look at faithfulness. Everything will begin to clear up when you do.

Tip: The real key to life is faithfulness.

17

The only way things are going to change for me is when I change!

Years ago when I was in graduate school, one of my professors was a psychiatrist named Dr. Paul Meier. He was an excellent teacher and always had a lot of interesting stories to tell. He taught us by using case studies. We learned the process of seeing how a person oftentimes creates his or her own problems by making poor choices or bad decisions. He also taught us how a person could begin to turn things around by learning to think differently and then making wiser choices and good decisions. I remember thinking to myself how much I wish I had taken his class when I was much younger, so I could have avoided some of my "blunders!" Unfortunately, most of us learn our best lessons from our own failures or mistakes. As I have often said, "Life is a great teacher."

I once asked Dr. Meier why psychiatrists were called "shrinks." He told me that a psychiatrist's job is to make you look at yourself. A psychiatrist holds a mirror in front of you and regardless of which way you turn, the doctor keeps holding the mirror in front of your face until you "shrink" down to the place that you are willing to face your own inner self and make some necessary changes. In other words, it is helping a person get out of denial and begin to think differently, which is a very, very difficult process. The Bible calls it repentance, and no one really wants to repent! Yet, it is the key to a happy, healthy, successful life.

I do not know if you have ever heard of the law of correspondence. It says, "As within... so without." In other words, your outer world is a reflection of your inner world. Your outer world is like a 360 degree mirror. Wherever you look, you see yourself reflected back. You have heard the old saying, "Wherever you go...there you are!" This truth is one of the greatest truths in all of human history. It is the basis for all religion, all metaphysics, all psychology, all psychiatry and all philosophy. It stems from the basic truth that if you can change what is going on inside of your mind (in your inner world), then you can dramatically change what is taking place outside of your mind, that is, in your outer world. In other words, your outer world merely expresses your thoughts, your dreams, goals, hopes, feelings and so on. That is why in many cases, what a person thinks about and talks about is what they actually "bring about" in the end. I am not talking about "name it and claim it" or "blab it and grab it." I am talking about asking, seeking and knocking for what you want to see happen in your own life. These are the keys to seeing your future go in a new direction.

Successful people are very clear about what they want to do with their life and future. They are always striving and constantly straining to do better. Unsuccessful people are very "fuzzy" about their own life and future. They simply take life as it comes rather than seeking out what they are looking for.

The law of correspondence says that your relationships, your health, your income and every other part of your life are merely reflecting back to you on a one-to-one basis what you are actually attracting. Everything you have in your life, you have attracted to yourself because of the person you are. You can change many aspects of your life by merely learning to think differently and thus, changing the person you are now to who you want to be. In that manner, you will then begin to attract a NEW dynamic to your life.

I use to wonder why ten different youth directors from ten different churches could each bring twenty-five teenagers to summer camp and in less than one hour, all of the "rebels" from each different youth group could all find each other and start hanging out together. Now I understand. You find what you attract. It is the law of correspondence. I believe one of the greatest revolutions in modern times is the rediscovery that anyone who is willing to change his or her attitudes of mind can change the outer aspects of his or her life. However the flip side is just as true!

You cannot be angry, unhappy, ignorant and

frustrated on the inside and have a happy, successful, affluent life on the outside. However, when your inner world begins to change, there will soon be changes in your outer world.

Have you ever looked into a mirror and did not like what you saw? Well, it isn't the mirror's fault, nor can the external mirror do anything about it. However, you can! The inside person can see what needs to be done and begin to make the necessary changes.

This week, take a look around you to see what you have attracted. If you do not like what you see, maybe it is time to change yourself and start attracting something different. I have experienced this truth in my own life, and I can tell you firsthand, it is the only way to do life... the only way!

Tip: The only way things are going to change for me is when I change!

18

Sometimes you simply need to get a different perspective.

The other day, I was having lunch with a friend. He told me that the older he got, the more aware he became of how important it was to see things in their proper perspective. He said, "I have come to realize that very little of what I initially think is correct, actually ends up being correct! It almost always takes me several days to get a clear perspective of what is actually going on in my life."

As I reflected upon those words of wisdom from my friend, I realized just how right he was! Seeing the events of life in their proper perspective requires a lot of wisdom… and patience. That reminds me of the story of the little hut:

The only survivor of a shipwreck was washed up on a small, uninhabited island. He prayed feverishly for God to rescue him. Every day, he scanned the horizon for help, but none seemed forthcoming. Exhausted, he eventually managed to build a little hut out of driftwood to protect himself from the elements and to store his few possessions.

One day, after scavenging for food, he arrived home to find his little hut in flames. The smoke was rolling up to the sky. The worst had happened – everything was lost. He was stunned with grief and anger. "God, how could you do this to me?" he cried.

Early the next day, he was awakened by the sound of a ship that was approaching the island. It had come to rescue him. "How did you know that I was here?" asked the weary man of his rescuers.

"We saw your smoke signal," they replied.

It is easy to get discouraged when things appear to be going badly. But we should not lose heart, because God is at work in our lives - even in the midst of pain and suffering.

Next time your little hut is burning to the ground, remember that it just may be a smoke signal that summons the grace of God.

This week, open your heart and mind to the possibility that God is trying to teach you to see things from a new perspective. Step back, take a deep breath and let go of having to understand everything so quickly. Maybe what you are going through right now is going to help you learn the very lesson that you will need to know to get you where you need to be!

Tip: Sometimes you simply
need to get a different perspective.

19

Never live your life on the basis of what other people think, say or do.

W e live in a highly impression-able world. Everywhere we turn, there is someone trying to get our attention. Look at all the billboards and T.V. ads as well as newspapers, radio and magazine advertisements. All it takes is one celebrity wearing a baseball cap backwards, and everyone follows suit. From the clothes we wear to the cars we drive, someone is trying to influence our every decision.

Recently, I came across an article that reminded me of the fact that some of us want to be different. We do not want to follow the crowd. We do not have a herd mentality. We want to make our decisions based on what is right, not what is popular or politically correct.

The following words were written by author Kent Keith. The wisdom of these words has inspired souls far and wide for over 30 years. Mother Teresa so thoroughly agreed with these words that she hung a version on the wall of her Calcutta orphanage:

"Anyway: The Paradoxical Commandments"

People are illogical, unreasonable and self-centered. Love them anyway. If you do good, people will accuse you of selfish ulterior motives. Do good anyway. If you are successful, you will win false friends and true enemies. Succeed anyway. The good you do today will be forgotten tomorrow. Do good anyway. Honesty and frankness make you vulnerable. Be honest and frank anyway. The biggest men and women with the biggest ideas can be shot down by the smallest men and women with the smallest minds. Think big anyway. People favor underdogs but follow only top dogs. Fight for a few underdogs anyway. What you spend years building may be destroyed overnight. Build anyway. People really need help but may attack you if you do help them. Help people anyway. Give the world the best you have and you'll get kicked in the teeth. Give the world the best you have anyway.[5]

I like that attitude and spirit. It helps me to see the value of thinking for myself in spite of what other people may or may not do. Thinking like that calls me up to a higher standard; one that brings inner peace, joy and contentment in spite of all that is going on around me.

Abraham Lincoln once said, "Trying to please everybody will satisfy nobody."

This week, take a closer look at what drives you to make the decisions you make. Is it better to live your life by someone else's point of view, or is it better to live your life for a higher calling from above?

Tip: Never live your life on the basis of what other people think, say or do.

20

Everyone Matters.

We live in a great big world. I understand the population is over six billion. That's a lot of people. It is easy to get lost in a crowd that size!

Last year, I had the opportunity to go to China. There are about 1.2 billion people who live in China. That is five times the population of the United States. I couldn't help but think how easy it would be to lose your identity in a "mob" of people that large.

One of the most important truths any person can come to understand is that he or she really does matter. I know it seems like we don't at times, but the truth is we do. I don't know if you have ever heard the following scenario or not, and "I can't take credit for it," but I certainly believe it is true:

"Everyone Matters"

For want of a nail a shoe was lost,
For want of a shoe a horse was lost,

For want of a horse a man was lost,
For want of a man a message was lost,
For want of a message a battle was lost,
For want of a battle a war was lost,
All for the want of a nail.

Unknown

That sort of sums it up; doesn't it?

Do you remember when you were in high school biology and you studied the food chain? That was one of the first times in my life that I really began to realize that every little part of nature really does matter. If you were to eliminate one part of the food chain, it wouldn't be long until another part would have nothing to eat. This would soon have a "trickle down" effect. Sooner or later, it would affect you and me.

This week, why not take a moment to look at your life in a whole new light? Even though you are part of the food chain (ha, ha), you are more than that. Even though you are just a nail (ha, ha), you are more than that, too. You are a creation of God, and as Aunt Jemima used to say, "God don't make no junk!"

I think one of the most important things people must know deep, deep inside their heart, if they are ever going to be successful, is that they really do matter. I am grateful for life; I am grateful for the opportunity to share good news with other people, and I am grateful for you. Do you know why? Because I know you matter...you really do!

Tip: Everyone Matters.

21

No Whining Allowed!

Several years ago, someone gave me a button that I really have enjoyed looking at from time to time. The button says, "No Whining Allowed." It is a white sign with black letters, and it has a red circle around the word "Whine" with a red line going across it to indicate that… No Whining is Allowed!

All of us have heard whining from our children. Unfortunately, it often comes from us when we grow up and become adults as well. Whining is more or less an attitude of "Woe is me! Everything in life stinks! It rained cats and dogs, and I got one with rabies! It rained soup, and all I had was a fork!" Well, I think you get the idea.

The truth of the matter is that we all have our ups and downs. We all have great days and not so great days. The key is to learn not to whine when things do not go our way but learn to "bite our tongue," and give circumstances and time the space they need to bring about some necessary changes in our lives.

Years ago, I came across a poem about whining that pretty much sums up what I am trying to say. Although the author is unknown, I can assure you that it was someone that experienced this whole concept of being around "whiney" people. After you read this, whining will take on a whole new meaning:

Today, upon a bus, I saw a lovely girl with golden hair. I envied her...she seemed so gay...and wished I were as fair. When suddenly she rose to leave, I saw her hobble down the aisle. She had one leg and wore a crutch. But as she passed...a smile!

Oh, God, forgive me when I whine. I have two legs. The world is mine!

I stopped to buy some candy. The lad who sold it had such charm. I talked with him. He seemed so glad. If I were late, it would do no harm. And as I left, he said to me, "I thank you. You have been so kind. It's nice to talk with folks like you. You see," he said, "I'm blind."

Oh, God, forgive me when I whine. I have two eyes. The world is mine.

Later, while walking down the street, I saw a child with eyes of blue. He stood and watched the others play. He did not know what to do. I stopped a moment, then I said, "Why don't you join the others, dear?" He looked ahead without a word, and then I knew he could not hear.

Oh, God, forgive me when I whine. I have two ears. The world is mine.

With feet to take me where I'd go, with eyes to see the sunset's glow, with ears to hear what I would know...

Oh, God, forgive me when I whine. I'm blessed indeed. The world is mine.

Author Unknown

See what I mean!?!

I read that poem to a friend of mine just a few days ago, and when I looked up, he had tears in his eyes. I said, "Please remind me of this poem if you ever hear me whining again!"

Don't get me wrong, I realize that all of us have circumstances and situations that are difficult to deal with from time to time. I do not mean to make light of those times. I just think that we ought to keep things in perspective as to the fact that whining does more to pull us down in the wrong direction than lift us up in the right direction.

Tip: No Whining Allowed!

22

Nothing worth doing is easy.

Several years ago, I began to get involved in working with e-commerce. As most of you already know, e-commerce is the wave of the future. Actually, it is already here for most people, and in time, it will be a part of daily life for everyone else. More and more people are learning to surf the Internet, and with that comes more and more sales. Merchants are finding that there are huge business opportunities available through e-commerce and Internet shopping.

If you were alive back in the early 1950's when television first came on the scene, you were part of a brand-new phenomenon that was taking place in the world. In 1950, only about three percent of the people in American had a television set. Now, everyone has a television. (Actually, everyone has two or three television sets!) Before the arrival of the television, everyone pretty much relied on information from their radios. Now, for the most part, people only listen to their radios when they are traveling in their car or when their alarm goes off in the morning. Just as television replaced the radio, the Internet and e-commerce is replacing much of the way we have done traditional shopping and purchasing in the past.

The Internet is a new, fast method of communication that produces great results. It enables us to keep in touch with friends, family, business relationships and business sales. Nevertheless, using the Internet in general and e-commerce in specific, does require a lot of effort and energy up front before good results begin to occur. For example, anyone who has set up a web site or spent the time needed to learn to send and receive e-mail, has found that there are many challenges. There are countless things that can possibly go wrong. If you place one dot or slash or space in the wrong place while sending an e-mail or searching for a web site, your message is lost, the link will not work or the transmission will fail. That is the nature of the Internet.

If you are a normal human, at times, you will want to just throw your hands up in the air and think to yourself, "I give up. This is just too complicated and too difficult to figure out." But, believe me, the longer you work at something and the more focused you are, the more things become easier, as well as financially productive. It is just not possible for something that is worthwhile to come very easily, otherwise everyone would do it. "To the victor go the spoils." That is true not only in war, but also in business.

This week, let me encourage you to stay the course when it comes to developing a mind-set of acceptance towards this new way of life called e-commerce. Do not get discouraged when things do not go exactly like you thought they should. It is a process that takes time and effort. However, it does pay rich dividends and rewards to all those who are willing the stay the course. Even though I don't always like it, I am willing to stay the course. How about you?

Tip: Nothing worth doing is easy.

23

Practice the daily dozen.

L ast week, I was attending an AA meeting (Alcoholics Anonymous). As many of you know, about eight years ago, I met a gentleman who has turned out to be one of my best friends in the whole-wide world. He is a recovering alcoholic, and years ago, he invited me to start attending AA meetings with him. At first, I was not too sure about this idea, but because I trusted him and our friendship, I went to the meeting. I was amazed! Although there were many people in the room who were still suffering from the consequences of alcoholism, there were many who had found wholeness, wellness and peace. Over the years, I have continued to attend the meetings periodically. I have found, in that room and in that environment, something special that I cannot find in any other place that I have ever attended.

Last week, I noticed a sign on the wall. The sign

said, "Don't forget to practice the daily dozen." Then the daily dozen were listed:

Honesty
Hope
Faith
Courage
Integrity
Willingness
Humility
Brotherly Love
Self-Discipline
Perseverance
Awareness of God
Service

As I sat there and read the list, I realized that this was a wonderful list of character traits to practice on a daily basis. I also realized the fact that those qualities were actually the road map to lead the way out of addiction, and a life filled with self-destructive behaviors. I said a little prayer while I sat there. I asked God to help those qualities become a reality on a daily basis in my life.

I do not know if you have ever attended an AA meeting or not; however, the recovery community is not just limited to Alcoholics Anonymous. There are many other issues besides alcohol that people need to learn how to deal with in finding help in their personal life.

I am struck by the awesome fact that our life takes on

a whole new meaning when we begin to practice different behaviors. I know you have heard the biblical phrase, "You are going to reap what you sow!" Often that is said with a feeling of despair, because people use that Bible verse found in Galatians 6:7 to indicate that someone is heading for trouble from wrong behavior. But remember, the other side of the coin is also just as true. If we plant good seeds, we will get a good harvest. The principle is just as positive as it is negative. It works both ways – *for you* or *against you*. Therefore, it is truly possible to reap the benefits of sowing good seed. Just ask any farmer!

Let me encourage you to review the above list one more time, only this time, read it a little slower.

It is quite a list. I copied it down, and will keep it with me in my "reminder cards" to keep my feet on the right path. That plan might not be a bad idea for all of us. Wouldn't you agree?

Tip: Practice the daily dozen.

24

Be like the mustard seed.

At some time during our life, most of us have heard the expression, "You need to have the faith of a mustard seed in order to do great things." Actually, the expression comes from the biblical text found in Matthew 17:20-21 NIV, "I tell you the truth, if you have faith as small as a mustard seed, you can say to this mountain, 'Move from here to there,' and it will move."

Those sound like some pretty lofty words to me. It also sounds like some power that I would like to possess. Anyone who has that kind of faith will certainly be a success in every area of life.

Over the years, I have often thought about what "mustard-seed faith" is really all about. I realize one of the facts concerning mustard seeds is that they are very small. So, one of the implications is that even if you have small faith to start with, it can grow in time to become the size of a mountain. Although I think that is a good interpretation, I believe there is something deeper being said here.

The one thing that is true about a mustard seed is that when it is planted in good soil, it is able to bring forth a mustard plant. The life of the tree is found in the seed. Because the seed knows its purpose, when it is planted, it brings forth fruit and produces after the way it was designed to produce. I believe that is what the story about the mustard seed is really all about. Once you discover the purpose for which you were created, and start to fulfill it, you begin to find your life fruitful, productive and fulfilling!

As many of you know, I believe the DISC information is the most important information that people can possess in their life in order to begin to fulfill their God-given purpose and design. If you and I are like a mustard seed, and understand what our purpose is all about, we will then begin to fulfill our destiny and the purpose in our life for which we were created.

Let me give you an example. I once heard Zig Ziglar say, "Because I am a high "*D/I*" type individual, my personality prohibits me from working for another person."

I thought to myself, "How wise!" Every "*D*" type personality that I have ever met has a destiny that they are seeking to fulfill. It is part of their God-given design and make-up. They will never be happy or fulfilled working in a situation that they cannot either own, control or direct on a daily basis. It is just part of the way they are designed. The same can be true for all the other personality styles as well. The more each one understands the purpose for which he or she was created, the more each one will begin to enjoy life, find fulfillment and be fruitful. The mustard seed knows how to do that. That is why it has been recognized for centuries as the example that we should all emulate and follow. It knows its purpose, and it goes about fulfilling it on a daily basis. If we have that same kind of faith and attitude, then we will be as successful as the little, tiny mustard seed.

I want to challenge and encourage you to spend some time reviewing the information regarding personality styles. The more you know about each one, the more successful you will be. I guarantee it! I believe it is some of the most important information a human being can possess, because it shows you the purpose for which you were created and how to fulfill it. Every person that I have ever met, who is living out their dreams or fulfilling the purpose for which they were created, has tapped into the secret of the mustard seed. Have you?

Tip: Be like the mustard seed.

25

In order to do what you want to do, you sometimes have to do what you don't want to do.

Most of us have things in our daily schedule that we simply do not like to do. We do not like to do them for a number of reasons. Sometimes it is because we are not good at a particular aspect of life. Other times, it is because we believe we are wasting our time or spinning our wheels. Let me give you a couple of examples. (I know some things are going to sound really silly, but nevertheless they are true.) It really frustrates me to have to bathe and clean up every morning. It is a 30-minute ordeal that I have to do every day. It seems like such a waste of time to shower, shave, brush my teeth, comb my hair and get dressed. Can you imagine how much time you spend in a year doing those simple tasks? Yet, I have discovered that they produce good results! I feel fresh; I feel alert, and it affords me the opportunity to interact with people all day long.

Another thing that seems like a frustrating thing for me is going through my e-mails. I get 100 e-mails every day. Generally, 10 of them are important, but the other 90, I have to wade through, delete and put in my spam catcher. Again, it seems like a waste of time, but the ten important ones that I receive usually have something to do with guiding my life, my business and my future. I could go on and on with the examples, but I believe you get the idea.

What I really love and enjoy doing is speaking, motivating and encouraging other people. I believe that is what my talents and gifts are. I also enjoy working on new products that will help people understand themselves and others better. Those things give me great delight! However, the vast majority of my time is spent doing things that are needful and necessary, rather than fun and exciting. I have learned that in order for me to do what I want to do in life, I have to spend a lot of time doing what I don't want to do! Let me give you another quick example. As many of you know, we have produced a lot of products, including a lot of books. I am amazed at how much time can be involved in getting a book written and printed. When the books arrive on huge pallets, we unload the books and put them in the warehouse and inventory them. Then we have to pick the boxes of books up and label them and take them to functions or ship them out on a daily basis for orders. (I feel like I should have been working out with Arnold Schwarzenegger all these years, so I would be a professional bodybuilder.) It seems like most of my day is wrapped up in picking up or moving boxes of books.

I realize that I am overstating my daily box-moving

trials, but it is amusing to me that it is one more thing in my day that I do not want to do that has to be done. As I look back on it, it really only takes up a small amount of time in comparison with everything else that has to be done.

What I am saying is that I have to work on my attitude about things that I do not like to do every day. I tell you this to encourage you, because I would not be a bit surprised if you face the same challenge that I do. There are "nit-picking interruptions" that we all face every day, but they are simply a part of life. I once heard Charles "Tremendous" Jones say, "I wanted to get up and make an impact on the whole world, and I couldn't even find a pair of socks that matched in my sock drawer."[6] I laughed, because I knew exactly what he was talking about.

This week, let me encourage you to cultivate a great attitude towards the things that you do not want to do or do not like to do. If you do them long enough and refuse to let them get you sidetracked or discouraged, you really will be able to focus on the things you love to do. Life is a balancing act, and I trust these thoughts will help keep you balanced in learning to do the necessary things that come into your daily schedule, so you can end up doing the things you love...that give you passion!

Tip: In order to do what you want to do, you sometimes have to do what you don't want to do.

26

Remember to pray.

Some of you may read this *"Tip"* and immediately think to yourself, "Hey, I thought these tips were related to business and my personal success. Doesn't prayer just have to do with my religious beliefs?!"

I will tell you that although prayer does have a lot to do with your faith, it goes much farther than that... perhaps farther than you have ever imagined.

Regardless of how smart you are or how well educated you are, there will come a time when you have arrived at the end of your own resources. Besides, if you stop and think about it, our own resources are very limited to begin with! Which one of us can make his or her own heart beat? Which of us can create oxygen to breathe? When was the last time that you or I helped the earth rotate on its axis? See what I mean?

I have come to see that prayer is not so much for God's benefit as it is for my own benefit. It clears my mind and aligns me to start receiving the good things that God wants me to experience in the bigger scheme of things.

Recently, I came across an old article that I have kept for many years. The story is told of a young confederate soldier who was found dead in a field after the Civil War. Someone went through his pockets and found this prayer written on a piece of paper:

I prayed to God for strength that I might be able to achieve,
But I was given weakness that I might learn humbly to obey.

I prayed for riches that I might be happy,
But I was given poverty that I might be wise.

I prayed for health that I might do great things,
But I was given infirmities that I might do better things.

I prayed for power that I might have the praise of all men,
But I was given weakness that I might feel the need of God.

I prayed to God for all things that I might enjoy life,
But I was given life that I might enjoy all things.

I got nothing I prayed for but everything I hoped for,
And despite myself, my unspoken prayer was answered.

See what I mean? In the end, his heart was aligned with a greater purpose than he first thought. That is what a prayer will do to you. It will make you a better person, seeing a whole lot more than you ever imagined… in your business, family and personal life. You may not get exactly what you pray for, but you will get everything you hope for! It's a guarantee!

Tip: Remember to pray.

27

I'm responsible.

I do not know if you have watched any episodes of the popular T.V. show, *The Apprentice* or not, but it is one very interesting show. Personally, I do not watch very much T.V., because I feel it is a colossal waste of time. However, I do enjoy shows that reveal a lot of interesting facts and data about personality styles, because that is my favorite topic! Perhaps no other show reveals so quickly how different personality styles do or do not work together with each other as this show does. Also, because this show is business oriented, I believe it demonstrates why millions and millions of dollars are lost each year due to one simple reason, namely, people do not know how to get along with one another. Even more amazingly, most of the participants on *The Apprentice* have graduated at the top of their class from an Ivy League school, and very few, if any, demonstrate a basic understanding of personality styles. It seems the only two techniques each one specializes in are power and being loud. Those two techniques work well in athletics and the military but are dinosaurs for today's business climate, family relationships and spiritual growth.

Anyway... back to *The Apprentice*. Each week the winning team gets a special reward. Last week, the winning team got to spend some time with former New York Mayor Rudolph Giuliani. (Because of his high profile in the 9-11 incident, he has become a public icon relative to leadership.) Something happened in that interview that caught my attention. On Rudy's desk was a name sign that looked like it would be used for his own name and title. However, rather than reading what I expected - Rudolph Giuliani, Mayor, New York City - the sign simply read, "I'm Responsible." Just two simple words, but those two words spoke volumes.

Mr. Giuliani explained to the young group of business-minded candidates that real leadership and success all boiled down to that one simple concept. It does absolutely no good to try and blame someone else for all of the failures, misunderstandings or mix-ups that take place in one's life each day. When you make a mental shift to the place of, "This is my job, my opportunity and my responsibility," then and only then will everything begin to change.

My mind drifted back to the time that I overheard Truett Cathy, founder of the Chick-fil-A restaurant chain, talking to a group of young people about success. He said, "If your job is cleaning the restrooms, then make those restrooms shine. Have the nicest restrooms that can be found anywhere. If that is your attitude, it will not be long before you get promoted. Your boss will see your quality of responsibility and will not be able to leave you doing that simple task. You will be promoted often and far. The cream always rises to the top!"[7]

Do you know how valuable that advice really is? Have you ever moved to the place of real personal responsibility... in your job or in your family? Have you really stopped blaming other people and decided you would fix the problem yourself rather than going on and on complaining about it to other people? When a person chooses to follow that advice, it makes a profound difference in his or her own life. It is an attitude shift that very few are ready to embrace. I find that odd, because on the other side of that attitude shift is reward, blessing and success.

Finally, I am not talking about being addicted to control and power. There is much for which you are not responsible and have no control over whatsoever. I am simply talking about being responsible for what is right in front of you today. What can you do to make a small difference in your own life that, in turn, will have an effect on the lives of other people where you work or with whom you live?

Patrick Henry once said, "I know not what course others may take; but as for me, give me liberty or give me death."

In Deuteronomy 30:19 NIV, Moses gave a message from God that said, "This day I call heaven and earth as witnesses against you that I have set before you life and death, blessings and curses. Now choose life, so that you and your children may live."

Rudolph Giuliani said, "I'm responsible."

Basically, all three of these quotes say the same thing! This is a powerful truth. Perhaps it is a good time for you to make up your own mind regarding what to do about this issue!

Tip: I'm responsible.

28

Memorize your favorite poem.

Years ago when I was in elementary school, I was introduced to poetry. It seemed pretty boring. It was all so academic. I didn't understand a lot about it at the time. I now realize that it was taught to me more like a science rather than an art. For example, I remember learning all about rhyming and cadence and alliteration and onomatopoeia. (Wow! That is the first time I have used that word in a long time!)

After I got to high school, I had a speech teacher by the name of Miss Julia Elliott. (She was the Griffin, Georgia, school teacher who won the contest for naming the new Atlanta NFL football franchise back in the 1960's... the Atlanta Falcons.) She was the one who introduced me to a writer by the name of Rudyard Kipling. I remember the first time that I read some of his poetry. To me, it was different. It was full of life and emotion and excitement. Perhaps that is why I was attracted to it so much. It kept my attention.

Then one day it happened. . . I read a Rudyard Kipling poem entitled "If."

"If"

If you can keep your head when all about you
Are losing theirs and blaming it on you;
If you can trust yourself when all men doubt you,
But make allowance for their doubting too;
If you can wait and not be tired by waiting,
Or being lied about, don't deal in lies,
Or being hated, don't give way to hating,
And yet don't look too good, nor talk too wise:

If you can dream – and not make dreams your master,
If you can think – and not make thoughts your aim;
If you can meet with Triumph and Disaster
And treat those two imposters just the same;
If you can bear to hear the truth you've spoken
Twisted by knaves to make a trap for fools,
Or watch the things you gave your life to, broken,
And stoop and build'em up with worn-out tools:

If you can make one heap of all your winnings
And risk it all on one turn of pitch-and toss,
And lose, and start again at your beginnings
And never breathe a word about your loss;

If you can force your heart and nerve and sinew
To serve your turn long after they are gone,
And so hold on when there is nothing in you
Except the Will which says to them: "Hold on!";

If you can talk with crowds and keep your virtue,
Or walk with kings – nor lose the common touch;
If neither foes nor loving friends can hurt you;
If all men count with you, but none too much;
If you can fill the unforgiving minute
With sixty seconds' worth of distance run -
Yours is the Earth and everything that's in it,
And – which is more – you'll be a Man, my son!

I read that poem so many times that it soon became a part of my life. Little did I know then the depths of wisdom that were contained in those few lines. Still, to this day, I find myself driving down the road quoting the lines found in that poem. Without giving you a line by line commentary on my personal experience, let me mention just one point: "If you can talk with crowds and keep your virtue or walk with kings – nor lose the common touch." After all these years of speaking, traveling around the world, meeting Presidents, senators, world-famous movie stars, millionaires, etc. etc., I still am grateful just to be a regular guy meeting people and trying to help people have a better life. It is just that simple! And you know what? I believe Rudyard Kipling was the same way! Even though I never met him, he could not have penned those words without understanding that concept.

Let me encourage you to read the entire poem and see the depths of wisdom found in a few lines of good old poetry. Who knows? It may be the one you want to commit to memory, like I did so long ago.

Tip: Memorize your favorite poem.

29

Be creative with your communication skills.

Have you ever read something that was so weird and "off the wall" that it actually made good sense? Sometimes that is what it takes to get our attention. When you always say the same thing in the same old way over and over again, people can become dull in their hearing ability. However, when you spice it up with a little humor and wit, then all of a sudden, you can begin to get other people's attention and drive home a point that might otherwise have gone unnoticed.

Hold on... I am coming to it in just a few more sentences! I just wanted to stress the point that taking a few extra minutes to say something in an extraordinary manner may cause the listener to get your point in a new and fresh way.

I remember when I was growing up, my Uncle Everett from Pennsylvania would come to Georgia every few years. He loved fish! So, my mother (his sister) would always get some fresh "red snapper," and we would all enjoy a great dinner together. One night after dinner, he wrote my mother a thank - you note: "The meal was nutritious and delicious and makes me feel ambitious!" That was over 40 years ago, and I still remember that thank - you note. So does my mother!

It would have been just as easy to say, "Thank you. That was a great dinner." But, he wanted to say more than that. He wanted to say something special. He wanted to get my mother's attention in a way that she would get the message that he really liked the meal! I believe he accomplished his goal.

All of us who have children want them to learn personal responsibility. Unfortunately, it is often difficult to communicate that message in creative ways. We tend to just say the same thing over and over. Recently, I came across an article which demonstrates how to say the same thing in a much more creative way. I thought I would share it with you.

This is a story about four people named Everybody, Somebody, Anybody and Nobody. There was an important job to be done, so Everybody was sure that Somebody would do it. Anybody could have done it, but Nobody did it. Somebody got angry about that, because it was Everybody's job. Everybody thought Anybody could do it, but Nobody realized that Everybody wouldn't do it. It ended up that Everybody blamed Somebody when Nobody did what Anybody could have done. *

See what I mean? Saying the above information in the way it was stated, sure beats saying, "Hey, would everyone around here start being more responsible for his or her own actions?!"

This week, spend a little more time being creative in your communication skills. It greatly raises listening levels and besides, it is fun to watch the reactions of other people when they hear the same old information in a new, fresh way!

Tip: Be creative with your communication skills.

*Author unknown

30

Focus on preparing not repairing.
(As it relates to doing a task)
Note: This is part one of a two-part series.

When I was growing up, I was a member of the Boy Scouts of America. I participated for a few years, but eventually I got tired of it. I now realize that it was a wonderful experience, but it was far more task-oriented than I wanted to handle. I wish I had that opportunity again. Now that I understand myself better, I would have stuck with it a lot longer. The people I have met who made it all the way to the rank of Eagle Scout are special individuals!

The motto of the Boy Scouts is very simple, "Be Prepared." As a child, I had no idea how valuable that one concept would turn out to be! You see, being prepared can save you a lot of headaches. It can make you a lot of money! It can lower your stress level and greatly increase your productivity level. But, learning to actually "Be Prepared" takes time. It is both an art and a science. It is something most of us learn through a lot of trial and error.

When we approach any area of life with a "preparing" mentality, something inside of us will change. We will be more careful to approach situations with the end in mind. Allow me to use a simple example that will illustrate what I am trying to explain.

Recently, I was mailing a friend of mine a package. I had written down his address, but I had forgotten to include his zip code. I could not figure out why I had everything except his zip code. Why would I have taken the time to write down his entire address and forget to add his zip code? Well, I had to stop everything that I was doing and go back through notes and old files just to find his zip code. When I finally found it, I added it to my current records, so I will have it for future use. That is called "preparing."

How many times have you taken the time to get someone's phone number only to need it again in a few days, and you did not save it? How many times have you talked to someone in customer service and gotten everything settled, but, when you called back, you didn't have the name of the person who helped you last time! We have all done that.

When you have to stop and straighten out situations, it is frequently because you have not yet developed a "preparing" mind-set. A "preparing" attitude looks forward into the future and sees many different possibilities. It sees what could go right. It also sees what could possibly go wrong. It prepares for the unknown.

It takes different options into account and tries to make every situation turn out as successfully as possible. In other words, it all boils down to the motto of the Boy Scouts... "Be Prepared!"

This week, take a closer look at your own thought processes or your lack of them! If you find yourself doing a lot of "repairing," the real problem may be that you have not developed a "preparing" mentality. A "preparing" mentality will, in many cases, help you to eliminate many of your daily challenges. This is an important tip that has saved my neck many times and will save yours as well.

Tip: Focus on preparing not repairing.

Focus on preparing not repairing.
(As it relates to building a relationship)
Note: This is part two of a two-part series.

All of us make mistakes. All of us have been wronged by another person, and all of us have been the one who wronged another person. It works both ways. When there is "wrong" in the area of a relationship, I believe we should do something about it as quickly as possible.

When we wake up to the fact that we have actually wronged or hurt another person, I believe we should do everything in our power to make things right. Sometimes that means an apology. Other times, it may mean restitution of some sort. In either case, when we have hurt another person, whether accidentally or deliberately, we should do what we can do to try to bring healing and closure to the issue. All of that is called "repairing."

I realize that relationships and interactions with other people can sometimes be fragile. That is why it is necessary to try to be upbeat, positive and as careful as possible when dealing with others. In that manner, you will have to do very little repairing. If you "start out" with an effort to keep lines of communication open, you probably will not "end up" in a mess! All of that is called developing a mind-set of "preparing."

Years ago, I had a good friend, Bill Vestal, who taught me a very important lesson about this principle of preparing in relationships rather than repairing. One day, Bill and I were having lunch. He told me how difficult it was for him to apologize to someone when he had done something wrong. He said, "I absolutely hate having to go to someone that I have offended and humble myself and ask the person to please forgive me." But then he said something that had a profound impact upon my life. He said, "As a matter of fact, that is one of the main motivations that helps me to not offend or hurt another person in the first place."

I was a little confused, so I asked him to clarify what he meant. He said, "When I am dealing with people, I think about the possibility of offending them or hurting their feelings. I also know if I do, I will feel badly about it in a few days and have to go back and make things right. And I really do not want to have to do that. Therefore, I work extra hard preparing on the front end, so I can keep things right to begin with. Then I will not have to do so much damage repairing on the back end!"

I got it! I understood what he was talking about. That was the day that I moved from "repairing" to "preparing" in my attitude toward other people and relationships. I began to put forth twice as much effort in the area of patience, love, listening and caring, so I would not have to spend time repairing unnecessary damage. Again, I have not mastered this principle, but I can honestly say that I have had this concept as a major part of my thinking for many, many years. It has helped me a lot...a whole lot...and it will you, too!

This week, watch your words carefully. Watch what you say and do as it relates to other people. Remind yourself, "Do I really want to go back to people that I have offended and confess to them what a jerk I was?" (Perhaps that thought can help motivate you to do better in the first place!)

I will be eternally grateful to Bill Vestal for teaching me how to understand this principle. It has helped me thousands of times...and it will you, too!

Tip: Focus on preparing not repairing.

32

Success in life all boils down to two simple keys.

I will admit it. I am a simple-minded person. There is a lot that goes on all around me every day that I often miss. I sometimes feel like I am still learning how to "connect the dots" in many different situations.

I like to reduce things to their lowest common denominator. That way I can remember things better. It makes more sense to my mind, if I can actually understand and see what is going on all around me. I am learning every day that there are good reasons why some things work well. There are also good reasons why other things do not work well.

Recently, I have been thinking a lot about life and how it all works. I have been talking to people whom I love and respect. I have been observing successful people who I know. I have been reading books about people who have made a difference in society by helping the world to become a better place in which to live. I have come to the conclusion that success in life boils down to two simple keys: having a good attitude and paying attention to details.

The first key is having a good attitude. This is more of an art than a science. When a person has a good attitude, he or she is a joy to be around. Even if things are not exactly how you would like them to be, if the people around you have a good attitude, it makes the experience you are currently going through a little easier and the load you are carrying a little lighter. However, all it takes for everyone to get worn out and frustrated is to be around a whiner, a griper or a complainer! Proverbs 17:28 NIV tells us, "Even a fool is thought wise if he keeps silent." Having a good attitude will open many doors of opportunity for you.

The other key is paying attention to details. This is more of a science than an art. I asked a friend of mine, who has done extremely well in the stock market, how he knew which stocks to buy. He looked at me and replied, "It is simple. Open your eyes and your ears!" I didn't get it. He went on to explain to me to simply watch where people shop, notice what people buy and observe what products seem to be popular and helpful. I started catching on to the fact that he was observing details in order to be successful.

Observing details has become a vital part of my life. Anyone who knows me very well will tell you that I always have a pen and a note card with me at all times in order to write down good ideas and useful thoughts that come to my mind. Paying attention to details has kept me from making the same mistakes again. I do not mind making a mistake. We are all human, and we will all make mistakes from time to time. However, I do mind making the same mistake over and over again, simply because I did not pay attention to what I was doing. That is unacceptable. Therefore, I have learned that I do not have to be caught off guard, simply because I did not take the time to double check my list or call ahead to get current details or get the name of the person who helped me, or because I missed some other small detail that could have made my life easier or better. I actually can benefit from the mistakes that I have made in the past or from the mistakes of other people.

This week pay closer attention to your own attitude and to the details that are taking place all around you. Success is not some vague attribute that is floating around in the atmosphere that arbitrarily falls on some people but not on others. It is the reward that goes to people who have good attitudes and pay attention to details! This is the truth if you have ever heard it. You can take this tip all the way to the top!

Tip: Success in life
all boils down to two simple keys.

33

Your vantage point will determine your outlook on life.

When I was growing up, our next-door neighbors had a giant tree. I loved to climb that tree! At the bottom of the tree there was a split. It made the tree fork in two different directions. One day, I found a rock that fit perfectly in the split at the bottom of the tree. It made the tree much easier to climb. Instead of getting my foot stuck in the fork of the tree every time I started to climb it, I could simply step on the flat surface of the rock and easily go up!

When I got up in the top of that tree, it seemed like I could see for miles. I could watch cars go by from up above. It gave me a whole new outlook on life. Everything seemed to appear so different to me. I felt this new sense of power. I have no idea why, other than I could see things from a whole new perspective. I would often sit up in that tree for long periods of time looking around, watching people walk by and yelling at people in cars as they passed by. It was always so much fun to me to watch people look all around to see who was saying, "Hi" to them. They looked to the left and to the right, but they seldom would look up. I guess when you are a child and you do not have a lot to do, you like to see everyday things in a new way. Climbing up in a tree seemed to help me begin to see the world in a different light.

Do you remember the scene from the movie *Dead Poets Society*, when Robin Williams stood up on the desk? His students thought he had lost his mind. But, in reality, all he was trying to do was teach his students to begin to see things from a different perspective or from a new point of view. It did not go over too well in the school and unfortunately, it still does not go over too well in life today. That is because most people are very satisfied with just going through life always seeing things the way they have always seen everything. They look to the left and to the right, but very seldom look up! I guess you might say most people forget the fact that somebody might have climbed up in a tree, and he or she is now seeing things from a whole new perspective. They themselves have forgotten the joy of climbing up in a tree and learning to see things in a whole new light.

Did you hear about the snail that was crossing the road on the back of a turtle? As he crossed the road, he could be heard saying, "Wheeeeee!" He was experiencing life from a whole new perspective!

The older I get, the more interesting life seems to become. I think I have learned more this past year than I have ever learned in my life. But, I said that last year as well. I guess it is because I am around so many wonderful people who help me to keep learning so many new things. Since I know there is so much to learn, I keep reading books that help me to see things and to learn things that I did not understand in the past. Someone said if you keep learning, it will keep your mind alert and will help you to live longer. If that is true, I will live a couple of hundred years!

Recently, I went to see my mother. I was walking outside, and I found myself drifting over to the next-door neighbor's house. I wanted to see the giant tree that I used to climb as a boy. I was amazed and disappointed! The tree really was not that tall. The tree had not shrunk. I had just grown. The rock I placed there about 50 years ago was still there. It was a reminder of my climbing days from many years ago. I walked away sort of sad that the tree was really no longer much of a challenge. Then I remembered that it was a challenge years ago when I was growing up. But, now that I am grown, I have new and different challenges.

Today I am still climbing, but it is no longer trees. Now it has become understanding business and people and capitalism and personality types and the Internet and e-commerce and international travel and trade and financial principles and investments and spiritual truths and creating new products to help families and starting new companies and motivational speaking and learning the publishing industry. It is a whole new perspective. One I find very, very interesting.

This week, start seeing things from a new perspective. Ask yourself what new information have you learned that has actually helped your own life to become better. In what area are you growing? What is the latest new goal that you have set for yourself in order to better your life or improve your situation? If you don't think about it, do you really believe your point of view will ever grow or improve? Maybe you just need to go climb a tall tree. That might not be a bad idea!

Tip: Your vantage point
will determine your outlook on life.

34

Sometimes you get yourself into a mess... but that's okay!

One of the most interesting experiences of my entire life happened to me in September 1970. I was living in Miami, Florida. I was asked to baby-sit for a wealthy couple who were going out of town for a week. They had five children, all under the age of twelve. I was going to stay in their house for the whole week. The parents left me plenty of money to take care of all the food needs for the week. There was plenty of food in the refrigerator, and the father encouraged me to take the children out to eat several times, as well.

At first glance, I thought this was going to be a pretty exciting week. I was staying in a very big house in Miami, Florida, with plenty of food and plenty of money to enjoy the week. The children were well-behaved, and I thought everything was shaping up for a good time. And then it happened!

The father took me aside and told me that he

needed to tell me a few important details. He explained to me that he was the president of a local political group. (Today I would describe it as an ultra-conservative, right-wing political group. I had heard of this group, but I was not familiar with their activities.) He went on to explain to me that there were a lot of people who did not like him. (Well, I did not think too much about that, because I knew that I liked him and his family and that is all that really mattered to me.) Then, things began to go downhill very fast. He walked me around the house and showed me where he kept all of his guns. He showed me the gun under the bed. He showed me the gun in the closet next to a large supply of ammunition. He showed me where he kept the gun in the kitchen, and then he took me outside and showed me the gun in the glove box of the car. I began to get a little nervous. Then he looked me square in the eye and said, "If someone kidnaps one of our children and demands ransom money, do not give them anything. Just let them kill the child that they have taken, but do not risk the life of another one of the children." If you think you are surprised by what you are reading, how do you think I felt by what I was hearing?! I actually thought he was kidding with me, but then I remembered the guns… and the ammunition.

Well, it was an interesting week to say the least. I did not sleep the whole time I was there. Every time I heard the least little noise in the house, I almost jumped out of my skin. I knew it was the kidnapers coming for one of the children!

The only bad thing that happened all week involved a phone call. I answered the phone and someone said the name of the individual who owned the home in which I was staying. Then he said, "I want to know if he is there."

My heart sank to my feet. I gave the best answer I could, "He has stepped out for a few minutes. May I take a message?"

The man then began to chew me out and explain to me the dangers of this political organization. I listened until he was finished, and then he hung up on me. Did I mention earlier that I didn't sleep all week? Well that night was especially stressful!

At the end of the week, the parents came back to their home. We were all glad to see them... especially me. I actually had a good time during the week, other than the fact that I was a nervous wreck. That was over thirty years ago, but I remember it like it was yesterday.

Sometimes you get yourself into a situation, and you don't know exactly what is going to happen. You have a picture of one thing in your mind, but it actually turns out to be something far different than what you expected. But, you know something? That is okay.

That was one of the finest learning experiences of my life. It helped me to realize that even though you may like an individual very, very much, he or she may be involved in something in which you are not familiar. That does not make the individual a bad person. It just shows that people are different and have different interests. I also learned a lot about this particular ultra-conservative organization. There were some great people involved in that organization. There were also some nuts! But, that is true in the church, in medicine and in every other organization. I also realized that whenever you start to talk about politics or religion, you are going to find a difference of opinion. But that's okay too, because politics and religion are two of the most important things in our life. We should all have well thought-out beliefs about politics and religion.

I can look back on that experience now and laugh. It wasn't very funny then, but it is pretty funny now.

Don't be upset at yourself when you get in situations that surprise you or catch you off guard. They can actually turn out to be great learning experiences and wonderful stories that you can later tell. I know that was the case for me!

*Tip: Sometimes you get
yourself into a mess... but that's okay!*

35

Remember your instructions for life.

All of us are human, and we all make mistakes, but we also do some things right, as well! As you have heard me say before: life is not just an "if only" experience; it is also a "next time" experience. I recently got a copy of a list of great instructions for life. Reading the instructions encouraged me to try to do better with my "next time" opportunities! There is a great deal of wisdom found in each one of these instructions. Again, this is a great list, and I wanted to share it with you.

"INSTRUCTIONS FOR LIFE"

Give people more than they expect, and do it cheerfully.

Memorize your favorite poem.

Don't believe all you hear.

Don't spend all you have.

Don't sleep all you want.

When you say, "I love you," mean it.

When you say, "I'm sorry," look the person in the eye.

Be engaged at least six months before you get married.

Believe in love at first sight.

Never laugh at anyone's dreams.

Love deeply and passionately. You might get hurt, but it's the only way to live life completely.

In disagreements, fight fairly. No name calling.

Don't judge people by their relatives.

Talk slowly, but think quickly.

When someone asks you a question that you don't want to answer, smile and ask, "Why do you want to know?"

Remember that great love and great achievements involve great risk.

Call your parents.

Say, "God bless you," when you hear someone sneeze.

When you lose, don't lose the lesson.

Remember the three R's: respect for self; respect for others; responsibility for all your actions.

Don't let a little dispute injure a great friendship.

When you realize you've made a mistake, take immediate steps to correct it.

Smile when picking up the phone. The caller will hear it in your voice.

Marry a person you love to talk to. As you get older, his or her conversational skills will be as important as any other factor in your marriage.

Spend some time alone.

Open your arms to change, but don't let go of your values.

Remember that silence is sometimes the best answer.

Read more books and watch less TV.

Live a good, honorable life. Then when you get older and think back, you'll get to enjoy it a second time.

Trust in God, but lock your car.

A loving atmosphere in your home is so important. Do all you can to create a tranquil, harmonious home.

In disagreements with loved ones, deal with a current situation. Don't bring up the past.

Read between the lines.

Share your knowledge. It's a way to achieve immortality.

Be gentle with the earth.

Pray. There's immeasurable power in it.

Never interrupt when you are being flattered. Say, "Thank you."

Mind your own business.

Don't trust a person who doesn't close his or her eyes when you kiss them.

Once a year, go someplace you've never been before.

If you make a lot of money, put it to use helping others while you are living. That is wealth's greatest satisfaction.

Remember that not getting what you want is sometimes a stroke of luck.

Learn the rules, then break some.

Remember that the best relationship is one where your love for each other is greater than your need for each other.

Judge your success by what you had to give up in order to get it.

Remember that your character is your destiny.

Approach love and cooking with reckless abandon.

Unknown

I hope that list means as much to you as it does to me. I would encourage you to post it somewhere and practice these suggestions. The list is worth practicing every day of our life. Wouldn't you agree?

Tip: Remember your instructions for life.

36

Take care of your health.

I am never sick! I eat fairly healthy meals. I get enough rest. I drink a lot of water. I get enough exercise on a daily basis. Plus, I live by the secret rule my father taught me years ago, "If you keep your hair dry and your feet warm, you will never be sick!" Of all of the truths I know, that is one of the most important wisdom keys that I possess!

Yet, in spite of all that, last week I got sick. I picked up a "bug" from somewhere. It has been so long since I even felt bad that I forgot how important my health really is to me. I mean to tell you, when you are sick, it affects everything! Food does not taste the same. I completely lost my appetite. Sleep was erratic at best. I would go to bed at night thinking I would sleep through the night and in two hours, I was wide awake! Even with medication, my body was off its routine, so I would be "up and down" all through the night.

A physician friend of mine ordered a strong antibiotic for me and that began to help. But, then I was warned by my daughter, Elizabeth, that an antibiotic kills all the bacteria in your body… the bad and the good. Therefore, she suggested that I eat yogurt to replace the good bacteria. Did I ever tell you how much I hate yogurt? I think I would rather stay sick!

The medicine finally began to work its power. That is when my fever broke. Then I was soaking wet! I knew that unless I changed my clothes, I would get even sicker. I ended up having to change clothes over and over in between baths.

I had also forgotten that when you are sick, you don't feel very motivated to shave or clean up. After 3 or 4 days, I started to look "grubby." But I felt so badly that I was not motivated to do anything about my appearance.

Finally, I turned the corner, and I began to feel like a human being again. My sleep became sweeter. I began to get hungry. Color began to come back into my face. I took a shower and cleaned up, and life began to return to normal. My zest for life began to come back, and I began to have a new appreciation for good health. I decided that I will not take my good health for granted the way I did previously. I also gained a renewed compassion for other people who are sick. Humility has been good for my soul.

If it has been a long time since you have been sick, I encourage you to use this tip as a "wake-up call" to refocus your attention to how valuable your health is and how important it is to be compassionate to those who are sick.

One final word: During the winter months, be a little more cautious about hugging and shaking hands with those who are sick. Be a little more aware of your surroundings, so that you do not get chilled or overheated. And of course, above all else, "Keep your hair dry and your feet warm, and you will never be sick," – at least you won't be sick very often!

Tip: Take care of your health.

37

Use the percentage road map.

S omeone once said that life is a journey. Anyone who has lived for some period of time could attest to the truthfulness of that statement.

Not one of us has a laid-out road map that we can follow day by day. We are all on somewhat of a "zigzag" course. But, that is actually part of the Creator's plan. It is at those turns in life that we learn the specific lessons that help make the journey a successful one.

To me, it is an interesting fact that the Bible says, "You do not even know what will happen tomorrow. What is your life? You are a mist that appears for a little while and then vanishes" (James 4:14 NIV). That wisdom was written 2000 years ago. Yet, it is timeless in its application.

Recently, I came across an "Attitude Percentage Chart." I was in a high school classroom, and I saw a sign on the wall asking the question, "What percentage are you in today?" (This percentage chart measures your attitude toward any task you might attempt.) Then the percentages were listed below:

Attitude Percentage Chart

0% - I won't.

10% - I can't.

20% - I don't know how.

30% - I wish I could.

40% - What is it? (Now you are open.)

50% - I think I might.

60% - I might.

70% - I think I can.

80% - I can.

90% - I will.

100% - I did!

As I read down through the percentages, I realized I was reading some real wisdom. Someone had taken the time to evaluate the attitude marks of movement toward success that any person would need in order to accomplish a task at each percentage level.

I realize these percentages could be used in a variety of applications. We are all better at some events than others. And of course, our own unique personality style causes us to be attracted to some activities more than others. At any rate, I started realizing that I was actually looking at somewhat of a road map that could take me from where I was in a particular situation to where I needed to be.

There are a lot of times that I have started out with an attitude of "I won't" or "I can't" and eventually ended up with an attitude of "I can" or "I will." Either of those attitudes will position me to move to "I did."

Let me suggest that you print out the percentage chart and post it on your refrigerator at home or on the bulletin board at the office. Watch people read it while they are reflecting on their own approach to their personal responsibilities.

Even though none of us owns a personal laid-out road map, this chart seems to help in the journey taking us from one point to another. Remember to use the percentage road map. It will help get you where you want to go! I hope this map will be helpful to you on your journey through this thing we call life!

Tip: Use the percentage road map.

38

Take the Test... to see
if you are a wise person or a fool!

All of us want to be wise. I do not think I have ever met a person in my entire life who deliberately wanted to be a fool. After all, being foolish is extremely painful. It hurts your relationships, your finances, your health and just about every other area in your life, as well.

I have discovered a quick little test you can take to see if you are a wise person or a fool. I thought you might like to give yourself this test!

Based on Proverbs 9:8, we can say, "Do not rebuke a fool or he will hate you; rebuke a wise man and he will love you." Well, which are you? How do you respond to words of wisdom? That, my friends, is the $64,000 question!

If you love to receive instruction, information or good ideas from other people and you also do not resist it when someone tries to correct you or even rebuke you when you are wrong (or even if you are right, you still receive it), then you are a wise person.

On the other hand, if you do not like anybody telling you what to do, if you are a "know-it-all" or if you resist it when someone rebukes you (whether that person does it right or not), then it is pretty safe to say you are a fool!

But wait – the test is not over. How can you tell how you reacted? I am sure we would all say that we believe we would fall into the first category and not the second one. So, here is the remainder of the answer key.

If you actually "receive" what was said to you and make a change in your behavior, then you pass the test. If you "reject" what was said to you and go on with your same inappropriate behavior, then you fail the test.

Inside each of our hearts is a "love-hate" switch. Some things we love; other things we hate. I love spaghetti; I hate boiled okra. I love warm weather; I hate cold weather. I love freedom; I hate slavery. I love capitalism; I hate socialism. (I know we are not supposed to "hate." I am not talking about "hate crimes." What I am talking about is things that we really, really like and things we really, really do not like!)

Just this week, I spent some time talking to a friend. It wasn't an easy conversation, but a very necessary one. He could have responded either way. He seemed to listen, but you never know how someone will ultimately respond. The next day, he called me on the phone to thank me for our conversation. That is what I am talking about.

There was the proof that he was a wise man.

Start taking a closer look at how you respond or react to words of wisdom that are spoken to you. Remember, however, I am not talking about words of stupidity. If someone advises you to go rob a bank, I would seek additional counsel. But, if someone tells you that you have a sour or rotten attitude, then that is a different story. You might want to consider that a little closer. And remember not to blame the person giving you the rebuke, even if that person does not do it exactly right. You can only be responsible for yourself and your own responses.

I have come to see the power of having friends who see things in your life that you cannot see. I am a better person today because of the faithful wounds I have learned to receive from other people. You will be, too.

Tip: Take the Test... to see if you are a wise person or a fool!

39

Double-check your backup plan.

A ll of us from time to time create a backup plan. It is part of life, and it is the wise thing to do. For example, most of us keep a spare tire in the back of our car. I do not think any of us get up in the morning, planning to have a flat tire, but it is wise to have a spare tire, just in case you ever need it. A spare tire is such a great idea that it comes as a standard feature on every car. I am sure, however, that all of the first cars did not have a spare tire. Somebody had to get himself or herself in trouble before realizing that having a spare tire would be a good idea.

Last week, our graphic designer, Pedro Gonzalez, had an unusual situation. His wife, Lisa, accidentally took his set of car keys to work with her. Well, that was no problem, because Pedro had a spare key that he had previously made for the car. There was only one, small item that he forgot to check in advance. He had never actually tried the key to see if it really worked. When he went to the car and inserted the key in the ignition, it did not fit. The key had not been cut properly. But since he had not tried it in advance, he did not find out, in advance, that his backup plan did not work.

When he got to the office, he looked at me and smiled and said, "I have a new tip for you. Double-check your backup plan in advance to see if it actually works."

Years ago, I read an article about a family that had a fire break out in their home. They had purchased a ladder for the second floor, in case they ever had a fire and needed to escape. They had thought of a plan and even had a method in place to protect their lives. Unfortunately, when they actually had to use the ladder, they threw it out of the second-story window, and they found that it was 10 feet short of reaching the ground. The length of the ladder was not sufficient. The family was forced to use the ladder, which saved their lives, but everyone in the family hurt their legs when they had to drop the last 10 feet to the ground. The good news was that they had an escape plan – the bad news was that they had not checked it out in advance to see if it worked properly.

Getting back to the spare tire idea, I want to tell you one last story. Years ago, my father and I were purchasing a car. The car had double white-walled tires. It was a very unusual design. Before we made the final purchase, my father asked me to look up underneath the car to see if there was a spare tire. I was dressed nicely, and I did not want to get on the ground and get my clothes dirty. I looked at my dad and said, "I am sure there is a spare tire under there."

Barney, the salesman, looked at both of us and said, "Oh, yes, I am positive there is a spare tire under there."

My father looked at me with his usual look and asked me one question, "Robert, would it hurt anything to look underneath and double-check?"

Well, he had me! I couldn't think of any reason that it would hurt. So I got a piece of paper and got on my knees and sure enough... it wasn't there. I was surprised, and Barney was shocked.

My father told Barney that we would not buy the vehicle unless he could find a matching tire to add as a spare tire. He looked all over the lot and could not find a matching spare tire, so we left without a vehicle. From that moment to this, I have always checked my backup plan to see if it actually worked - because, "It doesn't hurt anything to double-check."

This week, think about your backup plans and make sure you have checked them to see if they actually work. You might be surprised to find that they don't. Hopefully, you will be surprised that they do. After all, that is what this tip is all about!

Tip: Double-check your backup plan.

40

Don't confuse
principle with personality.

We live in a personality-driven world. The more popular, well-known or wealthy a person becomes, the more likely he or she will be to get away with just about anything. However, it can work against you as well. If people do not like you, or envy you, they can turn against your personality and really cause you some trouble.

What about you? Do you think people make their decisions any longer based on principle, or do they simply do whatever best suits their current set of circumstances and their own personality?

Most of you know that I love personality information. It occupies a great deal of my time and life. Therefore, because it is always at the forefront of my mind, I see it sometimes used in an unhealthy manner. Which one of us has not heard someone say to us sometime in our life, "Well, that is just the way I am!" What a sad way to live your life.

Personally, I do not think Abraham Lincoln could

get elected to office today. He operated his political life on the basis of right and wrong, not his personality style. He did not get up everyday; watch the news on T.V., then decide how to make popular decisions that would make everyone happy.

Each one of us lives his or her life based on some kind of standard of conduct, morality or code of ethics. Maybe it is something as simple as the Ten Commandments. (I like what Ted Koppel once said about the Ten Commandments, "What Moses brought down from Mt. Sinai were not the Ten Suggestions...they are Commandments.")[8] Whatever rules, regulations or laws you live by becomes your set of principles. If you live on the basis of simply what suits you today you have no principle... and that is bad for you. All you are left with is your personality.

Again, I love personalities, but only when they are accompanied with sound principles. Otherwise, your personality amounts to very little.

Some of you have heard me say it before...

"D"   What do you have when you have a "D" type out of control with no principle?
The answer is Saddam Hussein or Adolf Hitler.

What do you have when you have a "D" type under control with principle?
The answer is Colin Powell or George W. Bush.

"I"   What do you have when you have an "I" type out of control?
The answer is Chris Farley or Elvis Presley.

What do you have when you have an "*I*" type under control?
The answer is Bill Cosby or Oprah Winfrey.

"S"   What do you have when you have an "*S*" type out of control?
The answer is Magic Johnson in his crazy, reckless days.

What do you have when you have an "*S*" type under control?
The answer is Mother Teresa or Dr. Martin Luther King, Jr.

"C"   What do you have when you have a "*C*" type out of control?
The answer is Martha Stewart or Dr. Carl Sagan.

What do you have when you have a "*C*" type under control with principle?
The answer is Bill Gates or Tom Landry.

Again, it all goes back to one issue, namely principle! It is so simple. Simple to see it… simple to miss it.

This week, why not review your own set of standards, you own code of conduct, your own principles and see how you are doing. Maybe it is time to adjust your principles to the same importance as your personality.

Tip: Don't confuse
principle with personality.

41

Watch out for the guys who criticize and minimize the vigorous lives of other guys who visualize and energize and maximize an enterprise!

That is a mouthful; is it not? But there is a lot of truth wrapped up in those words.

All of us have known people who have encouraged us to try harder in our lives to keep going when things got tough, not to give up but to look forward to a brighter future. We have also known people who have discouraged us in everything we tried to do by throwing cold water on all of our dreams or nagging the life out of us over everything imaginable or by painting a bleak picture of the future.

It is difficult to admit, but sometimes we have been the one who has discouraged someone else. It is one thing when someone else is full of doom and gloom. It is another thing when we, ourselves, are acting that way towards others.

When I was in graduate school, I had a professor who was a genius. He not only taught us a lot of good useful, practical information, he also taught us how to think for ourselves. He gave us the key to know who to take advice from and also who not to listen to when they offered their advice.

He told us the following illustration. He said, "If you are out on the track running and someone is up in the bleachers yelling at you, telling you everything you are doing wrong, just ignore them. There are people full of bad advice and poor opinions everywhere you go. If, on the other hand, you are on the track running, and someone is running beside you, and he is sweating and aching and hurting and trying to complete his training program himself, and he offers you advice, it might be a good idea to listen to him. Why? Because he is 'with you' in the effort and experience. He has put in his time and done his own 'roadwork.' You might simply say, 'He has earned the right to be heard.'"

I am amazed at the fact that most people do not really understand that concept. Until you have actually been in another person's situation, until you have "walked a mile" in someone else's shoes, you really have little to offer that person. However, when you have paid the price yourself and gone the extra mile and have been committed to a task and stayed a part of the team, even when it looked terribly bleak, then you have earned the right to be heard.

I once heard a man running down his church – the pastor, the Sunday school teacher, the youth program and the offering appeal. He pretty much found something wrong with every aspect of his church. I personally knew he was not involved in any area of the church. As he talked, I could actually visualize him up in the bleachers yelling at all the people as they ran by! If he had been deeply committed to his church, perhaps he could have been the one to help make a difference. If he were involved in several aspects of the life of his church, perhaps he could be the one to help lead the church in a better or new direction. Sadly, I knew he had not earned the right to be heard, because of his lack of involvement and participation. He should just be ignored!

The same is true in business. Everyone can tell you how to run a business better until he or she has to run one. I have really learned this lesson the hard way. I used to have a comment or suggestion about everything. Now, I have learned that until I put in the time, effort and energy into a project, I have not earned the right to even speak about it, much less be heard by other people!

This week make the commitment to be an encourager, not a criticizer. It is so easy to find the negative. It takes more work to look for and find the good, the pure and the positive. Choose to be the one who rises above the crowd and is willing to help other people achieve their own goals and dreams. I have discovered when you do this, in the long run, it helps you to fulfill your aim, goals and dreams as well!

Tip: Watch out for the guys who criticize and minimize the vigorous lives of other guys who visualize and energize and maximize an enterprise!

42

Play like a champion today!

A few weeks ago, I saw a T.V. special about Notre Dame football. The athletic department, in conjunction with several high profile business partners, put together a "Dream Camp" for older men who never got to play football for Notre Dame. Most of these individuals are now successful businessmen who wanted to live out their dream of getting to experience what it would have been like to play football for Notre Dame.

They all got to get dressed in the real Notre Dame locker room, wear the real uniform, run out on the real field in South Bend, Indiana, go through all the drills, and so on! It was quite a sight to see! Many of these grown men had tears streaming down their cheeks as they imagined what it would have been like to actually experience playing for the "Fighting Irish" earlier in their life.

As I watched that television program there was one thing that caught my attention. As the players left the dressing room, there was a huge sign outside the door that every player could see. On the wall in big letters was the motto, "Play like a champion today!" The men were told that every player coming out of the dressing room should touch that sign on their way out to the football field. The players were told that there was limited time that each one would be out on that field each day. Their focus should be, had to be, MUST BE on playing like a champion for the next few hours. In that manner, each one could best prepare for the upcoming game.

I thought to myself, "What a good philosophy or mind-set that put in each player's head." Football practice was hard and grueling, but it didn't last forever, only for a few hours. If each player could train himself to do his best and to give practice his absolute all-out effort, he would get the most out of the experience. If, on the other hand, he went out and only gave practice a half-hearted effort, he would be setting himself up for failure when the time came for the real game.

I believe life is a lot like that. Each one of us has the same amount of time each day. If we work hard when it is time to work, we actually are preparing ourselves to succeed and win. If however, we only give our work, our relationships and our endeavors a half-way effort, we are simply setting ourselves up for failure in the long run.

Most of the challenges that we face only last a few hours. Some last longer for sure. However, I have discovered if I focus and concentrate on giving a situation my undivided attention and work diligently on it for several hours, everything suddenly begins to take shape and other events fall into place. To start with, it usually feels overwhelming, but in the end, it feels incredibly rewarding.

This week, start developing the Notre Dame mind-set. It seems to have worked wonders for them over the years. Perhaps it will for you as well. Maybe you could write that motto on a 3x5 card, and keep it somewhere handy to remind yourself of a philosophy and way of life that is hard to beat!

Tip: Play like a champion today!

43

When you know better, you will do better.

Al of us have made mistakes. Some mistakes are more costly than others. Dr. W. A. Criswell, former pastor of the First Baptist Church in Dallas, Texas, used to say, "You can make a lot of little mistakes, and you will be alright. But you only have to make one or two big mistakes, and you can ruin your life!"

Have you ever thought about why we make mistakes and how we can avoid them? I don't think, for the most part, we make mistakes deliberately. Why would anyone deliberately make a costly mistake that would come back to haunt him or her, or hurt him or her later on? The reason you made the decision that you made was because, at the time, that is what seemed like the wisest thing to do! As someone once said, "You did what you did then because that is what you knew how to do. If you had known better, you would have done better!"

I think the three areas where we make our biggest

mistakes in judgment are related to God, money and relationships. When it comes to the topic of God, you are always going to find that to be a hot topic. I heard Paul Harvey on the radio this week say that there are currently 40 different wars or conflicts going on somewhere in the world. Every one of them involves religion. I strongly suggest that you find out what you believe spiritually. After all, you are going to be dead a lot longer than you are going to be alive!

When it comes to money, almost all rationale goes out the window. All you have to do is read the paper or watch the financial news on T.V., and you will hear half of the forecasters say it is a bull market and the other half say it is a bear market. The truth is… no one knows. The only theory that is for sure is that the stock market is going to go up, and it is going to go down. That much I can promise you. I have found comfort in working with stable people who do not make decisions based on rumors, hunches, old charts or a good friend's advice.

Finally, relationships are where we all need help. Marriage, having children and life in general all come with very little instruction. Someone well noted that relationships are our greatest source of joy and our greatest source of pain. I believe all of life breaks down to learning how to have a good relationship with other people.

How would you answer the following question: "If you had a major decision in your life that you could go back and do over again, would you do it?" I am sure the answer is, "Yes!" I am also sure the decision would relate to one of the three categories: God, money or relationships. Don't beat yourself up. Learn from your mistakes and do better next time. Life is a long journey. The wiser the choices we learn to make, the better off we are going to be.

This week, seek wisdom from older, wiser people. Find people who are where you want to be and ask them how they got there. You really do not have to make all the mistakes yourself! You can learn from others, too.

Tip: When you know better, you will do better.

Learn to enjoy each day without having all of your ducks in a row!

I like to be productive. Everyone I have ever known who was successful had one thing in common: They made good use of their time. Because time is important to me, over the years, I have made a habit of writing down good quotes relating to time.

For example:

"Be a 'do it now' kind of person. First things first! Don't let grass grow under your feet."

Dr. Arlin Horton

"One today is worth two tomorrows!"

Benjamin Franklin

"Time makes more converts than reason."

Thomas Paine

"Lost time is never found again."

Benjamin Franklin

"All of life's problems can be summed up in two words: 'Too late.'"

General Douglas MacArthur

All of those quotes are good, and there is value in each one of them. The challenge for me comes when I am in the process of trying to use my time wisely by getting something done, and suddenly things begin to fall apart. Interruptions occur, the phone rings, someone drops in to see me unexpectedly, the car has a problem, someone gets sick, the weather suddenly changes, etc.! Well, you get the idea.

All of a sudden, instead of having all of my ducks in a row and events flowing smoothly, things begin to unravel. When that happens, I have seen my joy unravel with it. I do not want to be that way. I want to keep my joy even in the midst of difficult circumstances. I am just grateful that I recognize it and want to do something about it.

Here are a few things that I have started doing to help the situation:

1. Take a deep breath. That seems to help me get more oxygen to my brain and get refocused and centered.

2. Talk softer. That seems to help keep my situation from continuing to unravel.

3. Look to see what is actually taking place in order for me to learn and grow in the midst of the situation. My problem may actually be an incredible money-making opportunity trying to knock on my door!

4. Be quiet. When I am under a lot of stress, I am tempted to say something that is out of line. I give myself time to calm down and regroup.

5. Find the humor in what is taking place. After all,

in a few days, this event will become a funny story.

6. Above all else, remember that paperwork, events and deadlines have no real feelings, but people do. Therefore, I should be gentle with others when my ducks are out of line.

Now, I realize all of this may sound silly to you. But, I have lived long enough to watch myself and a lot of other people do really well when everything is going well but do really poorly when things are going poorly. I can honestly say that I can count on one hand the number of times that I have personally observed someone face a huge crisis, and he or she did not seem shaken by that sudden turn of events. I want to be one of those kind of people. Don't you?

I watched a fine Christian man go "berserk" in traffic one day when I was riding with him, because someone pulled out in front of him. (Now, I know that neither you nor I have ever done anything like that! I simply wanted to use that as an example to illustrate my point. Hmmmm?)

This week, watch your behavior, your words and your attitude. See if you get upset when things do not go as you had scheduled or as you had thought they should go. Implement a few of the techniques that I shared with you in this tip, and watch things begin to get better. I have watched these things work for me, and I am sure they will for you, too!

Tip: Learn to enjoy each day without having all of your ducks in a row!

45

Be enthusiastic!

I was recently reading a book that was written in 1949 on the topic of selling. I wanted to see what kinds of ideas were being promoted regarding working with other people. Since the book was written over one-half a century ago, I thought it might reveal some useful information. I also wondered if the ideas presented would be old and useless. Boy, did I get an eyeful!

The first chapter was entitled "How One Idea Multiplied My Income and Happiness." The whole idea behind the first chapter was increasing enthusiasm. The author talked about enrolling in a course taught by Dale Carnegie. As part of the course, he had to give a talk to the class. Halfway through his talk, Dale Carnegie stopped him and asked one, simple question, "Are you interested in what you are saying?"

His reply was, "Yes. . . of course I am."

"Well, then," said Mr. Carnegie, "why don't you

talk with a little enthusiasm? How do you expect your audience to be interested, if you don't put some life and animation into what you say?"

Dale Carnegie then gave our class a stirring talk on the power of enthusiasm.[9]

Mr. Carnegie made the point that night that by acting enthusiastic, you become enthusiastic.

To become enthusiastic – act enthusiastic.[10]

The author went on to say that was the moment everything started to turn around in his life. As a salesman, he found that the more excited he got about his product, the more he sold! He started realizing that his customers saw his own belief in what he was doing through seeing his enthusiasm ... and they started believing as well... and buying!

My mind drifted back to many years earlier when I was in graduate school taking Greek. We learned the English word "enthusiasm" comes from two Greek words: "En" (basically meaning in or into) and "theos" (meaning God or the study of God). Thus, the word "enthusiasm" actually means "in-God." That is the same idea as the concept that we are created in the image or likeness of God. The creator left his "fingerprint" on us to be like him – to think, reason, create, love, live, help, care and of course, be enthusiastic!

Earlier today, I felt a little down (because all the Christmas and New Year holiday excitement was over). Nevertheless, I started acting enthusiastic about what I was doing, and in no time, I started to become enthusiastic! This stuff actually works! That is why I wanted to enthusiastically share it with you!

This week, take a closer look at how you are acting. You will be amazed at how your feelings and attitudes follow your behaviors and actions. If you will follow this tip and add enthusiasm to your life by acting enthusiastic, you will definitely be pleased with the remarkable results!

Tip: Be enthusiastic!

46

You don't know what you don't know... but you can find out!

Every so often you will come across a simple story or illustration that will open your eyes to a new way of thinking. Have you ever heard a person say, "Then suddenly, the light came on!"? That simply means that he or she now understands something that was previously not understood. Well, I would like to share with you a story that has had a profound effect on my life and helped the light "come on" for me.

Dr. Scott Peck is a psychiatrist and one of my favorite authors. His book, *The Road Less Traveled,* has sold over five million copies. In that book, Dr. Peck discusses his thoughts on being frustrated with not knowing how to fix mechanical things. He writes, "Despite having managed to make it through medical school and support a family as a more or less successful executive and psychiatrist, I considered myself to be a mechanical idiot. I was convinced I was deficient in some gene, or by curse of nature lacking some mystical quality responsible for mechanical ability. Then one day at the end of my thirty-seventh year, while taking a spring Sunday walk, I happened upon a neighbor in the process of repairing a lawn mower. After greeting him I remarked, 'Boy, I sure admire you. I've never been able to fix those kind of things or do anything like that.' My neighbor, without a moment's hesitation, shot back, 'That's because you don't take the time.' I resumed my walk, somehow disquieted by the gurulike simplicity, spontaneity and definitiveness of his response."[11]   Dr. Peck goes on to write that those words impacted him and changed his attitude. His next opportunity to fix something mechanical (a parking brake), he actually took it step-by-step and succeeded in fixing it!

Dr. Peck, being a psychiatrist, saw the value in revaluating his own mental condition concerning the false concept that he had allowed himself to believe. For the first time, he realized that he actually could learn how to repair things. Although he felt it was a better use of his own time to pay someone else to repair it, he no longer believed the lie that he just was not very good as a handyman. He suddenly realized that by WANTING to learn how to do something, his entire attitude changed toward that new task.

I cannot begin to tell you the impact that simple story has had on my life. The part I like the best is when Dr. Peck stated, "I now know that this is a choice I make, and I am not cursed or genetically defective or otherwise incapacitated or impotent... I know that I and anyone else who is not mentally defective can solve any problem if we are willing to take the time."[12]

That story has caused me to rethink and restructure my own personal goals. I now firmly believe I can do better in several areas of my life where I previously felt stuck! The same can be true of you as well.

This week why not reconsider your own life and some of the challenges you face. Take the time to look at things differently. Talk to older, wiser, more experienced people who can offer you good advice to help you grow and learn the things you do not currently know. This in turn, will help you to become the person you really want to be.

Tip: You don't know what you don't know... but you can find out!

47

I love making decisions,
but I hate making stupid decisions!

Most of us make numerous decisions every day. It seems like my life is one constant decision-making experience after another. I often have prayed for the "wisdom of Solomon" in order to be able to make good, wise decisions. We have all heard the story of the young man who asked the older man how he got to be so successful:

The older man answered, "By making good decisions."

The younger man then asked, "How did you learn to make good decisions?"

The older man replied, "By making bad decisions!"

Over the years, I have analyzed the decision-making experience and have come to a conclusion. Most of us are normal, rational people; therefore, we should be able to make fairly good decisions. The problem arises when we do not have enough information to make a good decision. Therefore, the real issue is not "decision making," as much as it is "gathering information" in order to make a wise decision.

Let me give you an example. Recently my new son-in-law, Jordan, and I were discussing vehicles. I told him that I wanted to get a vehicle for my company. He told me that he was shopping around for a new vehicle for Esther. (Esther is his wife and my daughter.) Jordan is a real high "*C*", Georgia Tech graduate, who works for IBM as a senior CRM business analyst. In other words, he is smart. He spent several days researching vehicles and finally came to the conclusion that the best vehicle for Esther, as well as for my business, was a Chevrolet Tahoe. He then proceeded to use the internet to check all over metro-Atlanta in order to find the best deal available. I met him one afternoon, and in about 2 hours, we had purchased two Tahoes. Up until this experience, buying a car has been one of the most painful experiences of my life. Surprisingly, this car-buying experience turned out to be incredibly enjoyable. Jordan did all the research. He collected all the data and information. Therefore, when it came time to purchase the vehicles, it only took a couple of hours. Believe me, this is the way I am going to purchase vehicles from now on!

As you can tell from that story, the real issue in making most decisions is having enough facts and data in order to make good, wise, intelligent decisions. I still feel really good about the decision, because I have "shopped around" since making the decision, and I have found that we really did make a wise choice.

This week, slow down a little bit and look at the decisions you make. Do not focus so much on the actual decision itself, but instead, focus on the data and necessary information you need in order to make a good decision.

I believe the decision-making process for most people is a "cross your fingers and pray for good luck" type of situation. It really does not have to be that way. It can be a wonderful experience if we just have enough data. Knowledge helps us to make the best decisions possible. That one car-buying experience opened my eyes to a whole new way of thinking about the decision-making process. I hope it will do the same for you.

Tip: I love making decisions,
but I hate making stupid decisions!

48

Grow in your knowledge and understanding of "D" type traits.

Everywhere I go, after I finish speaking, I get asked the same basic question: "Dr. Rohm, can you give me a few helpful hints or tips as to how to quickly and more effectively read people?"

I usually respond with a few basic pointers like, "Look for outgoing or reserved traits in other people. Next, look for task-oriented or people-oriented traits." It usually ends there, simply because people cannot absorb much more than that in the beginning.

Over the years, we have put together a lot of charts to try to help people read other people better. Recently, one of our outstanding consultants, J.J. Brun, Director of our Personality Insights Canadian Division, compiled all of these charts into a simple format. He also added some of his own insights that he has learned from reading people professionally for the Canadian military.

Over the next four weeks, I am going to give you a copy of these four summaries in order to help you do a better job of reading people. I hope you enjoy these four special tips!

The "D" personality style is outgoing and task-oriented.

Response under pressure – Abrasive and tough
Approach to tasks – Do it now!

1. The Verbal or Vocal Tones of the "D" style:

   States more than asks
   Talks more than listens
   Primarily verbal, not written
   Makes strong statements
   Blunt and to the point
   Uses forceful tones
   Communicates readily (not afraid to speak out)
   Demonstrates high volume, fast speech
   Challenging voice tones

2. The Conversation or Speech Patterns of the "D" style:

   Limited…sometimes not even a hello
   Aversion to "small talk" or "chitchat"
   Attempts to direct conversation
   Dislikes "touchy-feely" terms

Under stress may become aggressive or defensive
Directive tones
Abrupt
Often interrupting
Often engaged in doing another activity during
   a conversation

3. The Outward Visual Body Language of the "*D*" style:

Firm handshake
Steady eye contact (if interested)
Gestures to emphasize points (finger pointing)
Displays impatience
Fast-moving body language
Dislikes being casually touched
Big gestures
Leans forward – advancing ("pushy")

4. Manifestations at the Office / Workplace of the
"*D*" style:

Full calendars
Pressure-cooker schedule
Likes to do things the fast way
Lets others know their time is limited
Frequently looks at watch – eyes shift or
   gaze elsewhere
Makes phone calls while speaking with you –
   while you wait

Walks fast, may not notice people around them
Few family photos (most out of view)
Workplace will have few "personal" distractions
Large desk
Awards displayed
Useful accessories

This week, be more aware of the people around you and the traits that they exhibit. Knowing and using personality information will give you the ability to relate better to every person in your world.

Tip: Grow in your knowledge and understanding of "D" type traits.

Robert A. Rohm Ph.D.

Grow in your knowledge and understanding of "I" type traits.

As I move through my daily routines, I have found it very helpful to remain alert to the clues that people give concerning their personality style. Recognizing a person's style allows me to interact with that person in a more effective and successful way. In this "tip," I am going to give you important information that will help you to quickly recognize the "*I*" personality style.

The "*I*" personality style is outgoing and people-oriented.

Response under pressure – Careless and unpredictable
Approach to tasks – Let's make it fun!

1. The Verbal or Vocal Tones of the "*I*" style:

   Tells stories, anecdotes
   Shares personal feelings
   Expresses opinions readily

174

Uses an abundance of inflection
Flexible time perspective when speaking
Variety in vocal quality
Dramatic
High volume
Fast speech

2. The Conversation or Speech Patterns of the "*I*" style:

Talks and listens in "feeling" terms
Uncomfortable with people who use sophisticated thinking words
Talkative
Varied tones
Often distracted with things happening around them

3. The Outward Visual Body Language of the "*I*" style:

Animated facial expressions
Much hand/body movement
Contact - oriented
Spontaneous actions
People will gravitate towards their space
Energetic
Poised and charming
Personable
Often look distracted

4. Manifestations at the Office / Workplace of the
    "*I*" style:

Décor reflects open, lively atmosphere
May appear cluttered / disorganized
Notes posted on walls with little apparent rhyme
    or reason
Furniture indicates warmth and contact – with
    extra couch and or table to accommodate
    conversation
Flashy and trendy with fun pictures
Likes to do things the fun way

This week, be more aware of the people around you
and the traits that they exhibit. With a deeper understanding
of each style comes greater positive interaction!

Tip: Grow in your knowledge
and understanding of "I" type traits.

50

Grow in your knowledge and understanding of "S" type traits.

L earning to understand the uniqueness of each of the four personality styles has enriched all my relationships. I know that all the attention that you give to learning personality information will help you to have better relationships also.

The "S" personality style is reserved and people-oriented.

Response under pressure – Hesitant and indecisive
Approach to tasks – Let's work together.

1. The Verbal or Vocal Tones of the "S" style:

   Asks more than states
   Listens more than talks
   Reserves their opinions
   Less verbal communication
   Steady, even - tempered delivery

Less forceful tone of expression
Lower volume
Slower rate of speech

2. The Conversation or Speech Patterns of the "S" style:

Natural listeners – prefers listening
Focuses on the conversation
Conversational
Warm tones
Very friendly

3. The Outward Visual Body Language of the "S" style:

Wears subdued colors
Favors conventional styles
Favors conventional vehicles
Intermittent eye contact
Gentle gestures (example: handshake)
Exhibits patience
Slower-moving body language
Comes across as reassuring

4. Manifestations at the Office / Workplace of the "S" style:

Personal and relaxed environment
Friendly and informal atmosphere

Organizational method – systematic and traditional
Will decide slowly
Will have items which illustrate relationships such
   as group photographs/landscapes
Family pictures and personal mementos displayed
Personal items which recognize hands-on
   volunteer work or hours
Likes to support and help others

This week, be more aware of the people around you and the traits that they exhibit. By gaining personality information, you will be able to develop relationships that are more positive, productive and enjoyable.

Tip: Grow in your knowledge
and understanding of "S" type traits.

Grow in your knowledge and understanding of "C" type traits.

G aining personality style information has been one of the most helpful things that I have done in my life. It has enabled me to become a better communicator and experience more success in each of my relationships. Interestingly, it is the "C" style that I naturally knew least about; and therefore, insights into this style have been the most vital for my life.

The "C" personality style is reserved and task-oriented.

Response under pressure – Picky and pessimistic
Approach to tasks – Do it right.

1. The Verbal or Vocal Tones of the "C" style:

   Fact and task-oriented
   Limited sharing

Formal and proper
Little inflection
Less variety in vocal quality
Less verbal, more written communication
Refer to themselves by given names...
   not nicknames
Speak in structured, careful speech patterns

2. The Conversation or Speech Patterns of the
   "*C*" style:

Asks pertinent questions instead of making
   statements
Speaks carefully with less expression
Reluctant to reveal personal feelings
Uses "thinking" words as opposed to "feeling" words
Prefers non-contact people
Prefers distance... desks separate you and them
Expresses themselves in a tentative manner
Likes speech to be precise
Will double-check on things/issues discussed
Silences indicate processing of data
Clarifying – will ask a lot of questions...they prefer
   more information
Monotone
Logical and emotionless

3. The Outward Visual Body Language of the
   "C" style:

   Conservative clothes with matching accessories
   Faultless grooming
   Unemotional
   Few facial expressions
   Few gestures – controlled gestures
   Slower moving
   Comes across as assessing
   Will retain their ground in stressful situations
     when they can rely on concrete facts

4. Manifestations at the Office / Workplace of the
   "C" style:

   Formal and neat environment
   Highly organized and structured desk
   Aesthetically pleasing
   Charts, graphs, credentials and job-related photos
   Pictures neatly on walls or shelves
   Favors a functional décor enabling more efficient
     work
   Most objects within reach
   State of the art technology to enhance efficiency
     such as planners
   Uses lists
   Likes consistent quality and excellence
   Decides cautiously

This week, be more aware of the people around you and the traits that they exhibit. I encourage you to continue learning new insights into personality styles. Learning more about personality information will enable you to create and maintain better relationships with each person in your life.

Tip: Grow in your knowledge and understanding of "C" type traits.

Stick with it!

Final Tip! **A** long time ago, I heard a very interesting story. It has given me a new way of viewing "hard to understand" situations. I thought I would share the following story with you.

Once there was a man who wanted to hire a young teenage boy to work in his shop. The first person who applied for the job came in, and the owner of the store showed him two barrels. One barrel was full of nails and the other barrel was empty. The owner told the young boy that his job was to take all the nails out of one barrel and put them in the other barrel. The teenager looked at the man a little surprised wondering what could possibly be the purpose of that task. Nevertheless, he started working. After about ten or fifteen minutes, he got tired of the job. He thought it was a stupid assignment and quit.

The next day, the second applicant came in and was given the same assignment. He worked for a little while, but again, after a period of time, he thought the job was a big waste of time. He figured that he had better things to do in his life than to move nails from one barrel to another barrel.

The following day, a third teenage boy came in and applied for the job. The owner of the store gave him the assignment. The boy quickly began the process of transferring the nails from one barrel into the other barrel. He worked diligently. He worked so hard that he began to perspire. After a while, he found it difficult to reach the nails in the bottom of the once full barrel. Finally, he got to the bottom of barrel, and to his surprise, he saw a twenty dollar bill. The boy picked up the twenty dollar bill and took it to the owner and said, "Sir, I found this twenty dollar bill in the bottom of the barrel of nails. It must have been put there by mistake."

The owner smiled and said, "No, I put it there, because now I have found who I want to hire. Not only are you a hard worker, but you are honest as well. You get the job. And by the way, the twenty dollars is yours to keep!"

I have never forgotten that story, because it teaches an important truth that most of us are not willing to accept. Sometimes we have to go through a difficult journey in order to find the twenty dollars at the bottom of the barrel. The process may make no sense at all, but that is totally beside the point. No one ever said that life would be easy or always make sense. No one ever said that life would be fair. We cannot always control situations, but we can control the way we work or respond when we are in a specific situation.

This week, let me encourage you not to try to figure out what is going on, but figure out what you can do in the situation to make things better. I promise you it will make all the difference in the world in your attitude and the way you do your work.

Tip: Stick with it!

Robert A. Rohm Ph.D.

End Notes

1. The Ruben Gonzalez quote and "The Champion's Creed" used by permission from Ruben Gonzalez – Olympian, Professional Speaker and Author of *The Courage to Succeed*. www. TheLugeMan.com.

2. This quote was taken from President Kennedy's Speech to the Irish Parliament on June 28, 1963. A special thanks to the Kennedy Library for information for this quote.

3. Helen Keller quote used by permission.

4. Gutzon Borglum quote and Mount Rushmore information used by permission of the office of interpretation in charge of Mount Rushmore.

5. "Anyway: The Paradoxical Commandments," © Copyright Kent M. Keith 1968, 2001. "The Paradoxical Commandments" are reprinted with the permission of Kent M. Keith.

6. Charlie Tremendous Jones quote used by permission.

7. Truett Cathy quote used by permission.

8. Ted Koppel quote used by permission.

9. Reprinted with the permission of Simon & Schuster Adult Publishing Group, from *How I Raised Myself From Failure To Success In Selling* by Frank Bettger. Copyright© 1949 by Prentice-Hall, Inc.; copyright renewed © 1977 by Frank Bettger, 12.

10. Ibid., 15.

11. Reprinted with the permission of Simon & Schuster Adult Publishing Group, from *The Road Less Traveled* by M. Scott Peck, M.D. Copyright © 1978 by M. Scott Peck, M.D., 27-28.

12. Ibid., 28.

About the Author

Robert Rohm is a world-class communicator who entertains as he explains key components to relationships and personal development. Dr. Rohm has profoundly impacted the lives of millions of people around the world through his presentations and through his books and tapes.

For nearly 30 years, people have listened, laughed and learned with Dr. Rohm as he pours himself into his high-energy, high-information presentations. He guides people into the principles that they need to improve their communication skills and leadership skills. He also inspires people to greater personal growth and development through his words and his resources.

Dr. Rohm has earned 5 degrees including his Ph.D. at the University of North Texas in Higher Education Administration and Counseling. Dr. Rohm has authored or coauthored several books including *Positive Personality Profiles, Who Do You Think You Are Anyway?, You've Got Style, Different Children Different Needs, Tales Out of School, Get Real!, All about Bots! All about You!, A+ Ideas for Every Student's Success, A Tip in the Right Direction Volume I* and *Volume II,* and *Praying for your Child.*

Resource Materials

A Tip in the Right Direction Volume I and II
Life is too short to make all the mistakes yourself! Learn real wisdom from the mistakes of others! Dr. Rohm shares a lifetime of experiences in these easy - to - read books. They contain valuable insights that will change your life, and it only takes a couple of minutes a week to gain this powerful knowledge.

You've Got Style
This book is a great introductory book on DISC personality styles. It gives all the basic information about the four personality styles, and it also includes chapters on adapting your style and building better teams.

Praying for your Child
According to his or her Personality Style
All parents want the best for their child. This book walks parents step-by-step into a creative approach to parenting that works with their child's natural style instead of against it. It blends the understanding of personality styles with Biblical principles to produce stronger relationships with happier parents and children.

As you read this book, you will learn how to motivate your child, how to discipline your child and how to truly delight in your child!

Discovery Report, (Online Assessment)*
(For adults)
This is a 40+ page report that is personalized just for you. Learn about your own personality style, your ideal environment, your blind spots, your communication style and much more. It begins with an online assessment. After completing the assessment, your Discovery Report is e-mailed to you in about an hour.

*Also, available in Spanish

Get Real! (Online Assessment for Teens)
This report gives you over 40 pages of specific information for teens. This is one of the most accurate tools available for DISCovering your personality style.

Purpose: This report serves as a guide (like a development handbook) to help teens gain insight into their own motivations, goals and outlook on life.

Description: A personality style analysis for teens designed to define specific personal self-awareness and understanding. The report also lists attributes and occupations associated with personality types. This assessment can be completed in about 15 minutes.

All About Bots! All About You!
(Online Assessment for Children ages 4-12)
This report gives you over 50 pages of specific information for children ages 4-12. This is one of the most accurate tools available for DISCovering a child's personality style. The information you receive helps a child and his or her parents learn about personality styles.

Purpose: To help parents, teachers and individuals who work with children to better understand them, and for the children to understand themselves and others by explaining personality behaviors and tendencies.

Description: Children look at pictures and read stories selecting the choices that appeal most to them. Stories reveal different styles of behavior. The information generated from the report teaches children how to relate to others as well as understanding the needs of other people. The vital information in this report provides parents and teachers with specific insights to help the child as he or she develops and matures.

L.E.A.D.E.R.S.H.I.P. By The Letter Audio CD

Get ready to laugh and learn with Dr. Rohm as he explains 10 principles to be an effective leader. Dr. Rohm give secrets on what it takes to be a "true" leader in every situation.

Multimedia/Interactive CD

This is one of THE most FUN multimedia presentations ever done for the computer. This inspiring presentation helps people understand personalities in a whole new and insightful way. You will find that it is not only fun to watch, but it is interactive as well!

How to Understand Yourself and Others-DVD

Two DVDs and a small workbook are included. There are six 30-minute sessions. (There are three on each DVD.) These presentations provide an overview of the DISC model. It is an excellent format for individuals to understand themselves and others while working on having better relationships and better teams.

We at Personality Insights want to invite you to come to our web site and view the many valuable resources that we make available. We specialize in resources that are particularly related to families, businesses, churches and schools. We also offer many other spiritual, leadership and educational materials. Also, there is a 3 - day training course held in Atlanta, Georgia that you can attend and become a certified Human Behavior Consultant.

Our resources can be ordered by calling

1-800-509-DISC

or visiting

www.personalityinsights.com.

Robert A. Rohm Ph.D.